Smile and Enjoy the Adventure

Smile and Enjoy the Adventure

JOURNEYS WITH MY HUSBAND

A 'Travel Log'
to the remotest parts of Russia

Carol Lay

Published by Mineit Press
Duporth Bay, St Austell, Cornwall PL26 6AF, England
Lay@mineit.co.uk

ISBN 978-1-9999948-0-8

Printed and bound by
Palace Printers, Quay Street, Lostwithiel, Cornwall PL22 0BS

DEDICATION

To my husband Stephen, travelling companion in life as well as in Siberia. All my love always.

To our children Tamsin, Naomi and Ian who conveniently flew the nest and were having their own adventures.

To our grandchildren Elowen, Lottie, Tom, Ollie and Sam, whose smiles gave me great strength. Enjoy your adventures.

To my family and friends who encouraged these ramblings.

To those we met on our journeys, and those who welcomed us into their countries, communities, homes and hearts.

With love …

FOREWORD

"I have had a rich life and I am who I am because of life's rich tapestry" wrote Carol in a book she contributed to in 2012.

What you will read here is a part of that rich tapestry as Carol evocatively and wittily describes her travels as she accompanies her mining engineer husband across Russia.

This book started out in 2001 as an emailed 'travel log' which she entitled 'Journeys with My Husband' and was sent to friends and family around the world. With positive feedback and encouragement, and the "have we missed an edition?" messages it was becoming clear that she was bringing a smile to many as she shared her adventure. The circulation list grew.

I'm sure Carol never intended for her musings to be published. '*Smile and enjoy the Adventure*' are those very unabridged emails, in her style and her 'voice', which tell the story of her adventures with Stephen in Russia and Kazakhstan. This was at a time when these countries were emerging from communism, adjusting to market economies and seeking foreign investment to develop their mineral resources.

Here you will find a non-judgemental and candid account of how Carol saw life as they lived and travelled in places where only a few Westerners have had the privilege to visit, let alone live. The difference in living conditions and climate could not have been more extreme compared with Cornwall in South West England where they were brought up.

This book documents their adventures, through Carol's eyes, as they travel to, and live in: Moscow; in remote Kamchatka on the Russian Pacific coast; in freezing Yakutsk in eastern Siberia and in eastern Kazakhstan.

Occasionally Carol would visit Stephen on his other international assignments, to: South Africa; Lesotho; Archangel in north-west Russia and Georgia in the Former Soviet Union.

"The unexpected can be expected" is one of Carol's phrases. Nothing could prepare you for the final chapter, a legacy of Stephen's work in Georgia, which stopped their international travel and adventures.

I was on that original email circulation list.

'*Smile and Enjoy the Adventure*'. I have, you will!

Enid Johns MBE, 2018
Helston, Cornwall, England
Carol's friend and mentor for over 45 years.

ACKNOWLEDGMENTS

This book started as a series of emails from Russia to Carol's family, friends and colleagues. The circulation list grew, and grew. Thanks are due to all those early readers who encouraged Carol's writing as she travelled with me.

Special thanks must go to Enid Johns MBE who, from the very early emails, has enthusiastically encouraged the publication of this book.

The maps have been brilliantly traced and coloured by our grandchildren Elowen, Charlotte, Tom and Oliver. Well done kids!

Special mention goes to all who have been part of our life journey, whether at home or abroad. Especially to Carol's very loyal friends and colleagues Val, Helen, Janet and Tony, all of whom shared her passion for children with special needs. To all our Rotary friends at home and abroad who knew and loved Carol and have supported us in the true Rotary way. In particular Sandra and Jill for their proof reading and suggestions, my thanks - any errors are purely down to me!

My grateful thanks to Martin Murray, graphic designer, who has performed his magic on the photos and cover. The original 'snapshots' were never intended for publication!

And thanks to you for purchasing this book, not only are you sharing in our adventures, but you are also helping a cause which was very close to Carol's heart. All profits are to be donated to Carol's Memorial Fund set up by Children's Hospice South West to support the siblings of life limited children. You are helping to make a difference. For more on how you can help see www.carolslegacy.co.uk .

Stephen Lay, 2018
Duporth Bay, Cornwall, England

THE FORMER SOVIET UNION

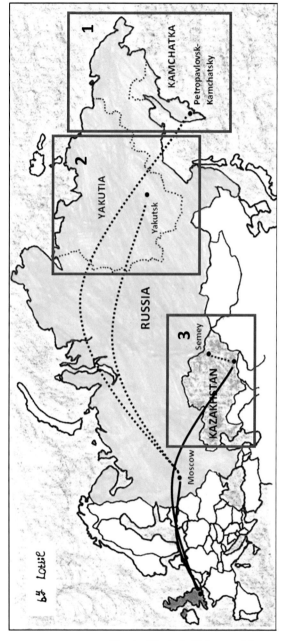

London to Moscow: 2,500 km (1,550 miles) and 3 time zones ahead of the UK

Moscow to Petropavlovsk-Kamchatsky: 6,750 km (4,200 miles) and 12 time zones

Moscow to Yakutia: 4,700 km (2,950 miles) and 9 time zones

London to Semey: 5,150 km (3,200 miles) and 6 time zones

Map by Charlotte Hahn, aged 6.

CONTENTS

KAMCHATKA 2001

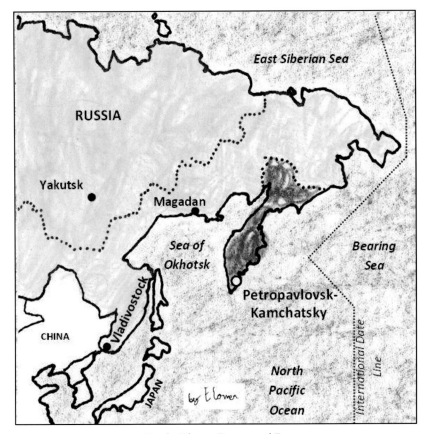

Map by Elowen Reeve, aged 7.

Carol and Stephen could not have travelled further from their home in Cornwall, England. Travelling due east, or west, the Russian peninsula of Kamchatka is almost literally on the other side of the world.

Nor could they have travelled further east in Russia as the Kamchatka Peninsula protrudes into the Pacific Ocean with the Sea of Okhotsk to the west. Almost 7,000 km (4,200 miles) from Moscow and with no roads to the peninsula, the region was protected by the Soviet Union as it was the home to a nuclear submarine base and other top secret military installations. For decades it was off limits to all but natives, sailors and fishermen.

Those familiar with the board game "Risk" may already be partly familiar with Kamchatka. Kamchatka is also known as the "land of fire and ice" and here you are possibly at the greatest risk from mother nature than anywhere else in the world: active volcanoes; earthquakes; tsunamis; avalanches; climate; bears and mosquitos! The population of the peninsula is sparse with the majority, about 200,000, living in the port city of Petropavlovsk-Kamchatsky (PK) in the south-east of the peninsula.

The economy of the peninsula largely relies on fishing and forestry with a developing tourism industry showcasing its unique and pristine features.

Although Kamchatka lies at similar latitudes to England it has a subarctic climate. Cold arctic winds from Siberia combined with the cold Oyashio sea current see the peninsula covered in snow from October to late May and the sea freezes. More northerly areas have a polar climate. Kamchatka is much wetter and milder than eastern Siberia.

Geologically the region is very active being on the Pacific Rim of Fire, the Kamchatka volcanic province is one of the world's finest example of large scale subduction of an oceanic plate with hundreds of volcanoes of which about 30 are active. The volcanos overshadowing the city of PK are the Avachinsky Volcano (2,741 m above sea level), Koryakskaya Sopka (3,456 m).

The Kamchatka Peninsula has only emerged as a potential gold mining province since the breakup of the Soviet Union. For much of the 20th century the region has been closed to foreigners and restricted to Russians. Exploration in Kamchatka by Soviet geologists started in the 1970's leading to the discovery of several epithermal[1] gold deposits.

Building on the earlier Soviet exploration work, and more recent western exploration, Stephen was contracted to develop the feasibility studies for the development of gold mines at the Asachinskoye and Rodnikovoye deposits at the southern end of the peninsula, 150 km south of PK. Gold production started at the Asacha mine in 2011.

In October 2001, Carol and Stephen travelled to Petropavlovsk-

---

[1] Epithermal deposits form very close to the surface of the earth at relatively low temperature and pressure. A characteristic of epithermal gold deposits is that you can virtually see them forming today by visiting hot springs such as on the Kamchatka Peninsula.

Kamchatsky via Moscow.

And now over to Carol, verbatim, her emails to friends and family.

32 ° proof!

NIGHT TIME GAMES

Carol Lay

From: Carol Lay
Sent: 13 October 2001 05:32
Subject: Russian trips

JOURNEY WITH MY HUSBAND
A TRAVEL LOG

Moscow, Russia
Thursday 4 October 2001

Moscow has changed quite considerably since my last visit five years ago. The city centre has all the trappings of any other large capital city; brightly illuminated stores, massive TV type adverts, well dressed people and some beggars. The signs of poverty are now far less apparent.

We had a good room at the Arbat Hotel and there was no feeling of anxiety when I went out exploring alone as it was a tourist area so people were not specifically watching me. I was delighted to see there were Gap stores until I realised that in Russian Cyrillic "Gap" spells "bar" but I was just as happy with that!

Out and about alone. Stephen at yet another meeting. I managed to purchase some postcards and pay for them, using lots of sign language and thankfully finding a sales assistant with some English. Purchasing stamps was a bit more challenging and it took me until late afternoon to pluck up the courage to go to the post office. No English speaking post mistress, but armed with phrase book and the corner of a postcard to point to I managed to get the right stamps to send cards to England and France and understand that I needed to put two stamps on each card!

On Stephen's return we went for a stroll around. Stephen spotted a sign for a Georgian restaurant where we just had to go and eat so that he could practise the half dozen words he had acquired whilst working in the Republic of Georgia. Interesting that they all related to food. Unfortunately, the staff in the restaurant were not Georgian but what was even more disappointing was that they couldn't speak English. Mercifully, because we were quite hungry by this time, the menu was in English! We were also fortunate that when we did stumble on problems such as not being able to explain we wanted a bottle of red wine, quite an important

4

fact, there was a lady sitting on the table next to us who came most ably to our rescue.

Saturday was rainy but reasonably mild and we walked to Red Square, had a cappuccino and wandered on past the eternal flame and about five different wedding parties until we found another coffee shop. Had more cappo and some delicious cakes. Then caught the Metro back. Decided to have KFC for our meal and then back to pack ready to fly on to Petropavlovsk-Kamchatsky.

During the night it dawned on me why there was a life-size model cow outside the Restaurant called "мy мy". In Cyrillic "мy мy" reads "moo moo"! Say no more.

We eventually managed to check out of our hotel after the usual hassle of being overcharged, "can't cancel your credit card now sir cos we whizzed it" but, you know the story. The staff at the hotel definitely were on a go-slow and there was dreadful service in the restaurant and café, but quite amusing as well.

Onto the airport. Calm down Carol! Russian airports make me jittery anyway, but we were supposed to be meeting somebody there but he was delayed so there was a dilemma, to check-in or not to check-in. It's backwards at this airport, security first and then check-in. My instructions are, "Just smile Carol." Difficult but I managed it! Eventually we're checked in and our flight is called. We get on a bus to be driven to the aircraft. What's unusual? Fifteen minutes later we are still waiting to move. One little toddler, after several attempts to get through the closed door persuaded his embarrassed mum to get out his potty as he was dying for a wee, and by Jove was he! When you've gotta go you've gotta go.

So to the plane. Aeroflot. Didn't look forward to this flight, allowed off the bus all in one gaggle only to be stopped at the steps. I got separated from Stephen and wouldn't go onto the plane without him. The look I was given was far superior to any Lay look I could muster, but she let Stephen through and we took our seats. Apart from a 25 minute delay the flight was uneventful, but the smell of the plane is indescribable, Yuck!!

Ten hours later, and one day later, it's now Monday, we arrived in Kamchatka. BEAUTIFUL. We flew over the mountains of Siberia and then over the volcanoes and mountains of Kamchatka. The airport took ages but eventually we were on our way to the Hotel Roos. Not quite the Ritz, well nowhere near the Ritz actually, but Stephen says it is much improved since his last visit. Heaven help us! We have a suite: bedroom, sitting room, hallway and bathroom. I can't describe the bathroom, don't know the correct vocab. It works I suppose and there is plenty of hot water, the rooms are warm, the beds are two, split by wooden frames and the smell is......

Next we go to the office, a typical Russian building, utilitarian, but okay, fantastic views from Stephen's office. Oh yes, and did I say we saw that the Avacha volcano (a few miles from PK) is active!

We finished work quite early, jet lagged; we are now 12 hours ahead of the UK. Back to the hotel, nearly fall asleep over dinner, so pick up emails and off to bed.

Not quiet! The phone rings in all the rooms, three times about every half hour, there are ladies around wondering if anybody wants to play some games. It sounds like some people do, and are!!

Early Tuesday we were awoken by an earthquake, nothing much, a minor tremor, maybe a two on the Richter Scale, and did I tell you another volcano is active......

To be continued.

The Avacha volcano looming over Petropavlovsk-Kamchatsky.

HOT SPRINGS

Carol Lay

From:	Carol Lay
Sent:	19 October 2001 12:26
Subject:	Journeys with my Husband: Part 2

JOURNEY WITH MY HUSBAND
PART 2

Petropavlovsk-Kamchatsky, Kamchatka, Russia
Wednesday 17 October 2001

Slowly our bodies are adjusting to the time difference, and noise allowing, we are beginning to sleep better, thus we are more observant of our environment, both in terms of human and natural!

The climate is not as cold as I had anticipated, there have been frosts and it is much colder than we would experience in England at this time of year, but it is easily bearable.

The scenery is spectacular. You cannot fail to be impressed with the natural beauty of this area, snow clad volcanoes which are gently smouldering into a blue sky. All this is set against the blue of the Pacific Ocean. As the light and weather changes throughout the day so does the view.

When we look out of our hotel room windows we can see two of the volcanoes. They form the backdrop for a wooded area, maybe it is a forest, lots of hills and mountains. On the drive to the office we pass through built up areas of high rise apartments, single storey buildings which are shops or offices and then you round a bend and see the volcanoes! Magnificent!

One evening this week, Stephen's interpreter invited us to a party. We were collected from our hotel and driven, rather erratically, to a dacha (country house) for the party. This house lay at the foot of the Avacha volcano and a light covering of snow lay on the ground. The man who owned the house, Boris, had apparently built it himself. It was made of timber and included a sauna, the offer of which Stephen and I chose to decline! We had a tour of the garden and green house: very interesting, really well kept and displaying many varieties of plants that we would expect to grow including strawberries, blackcurrant and gooseberry bushes. In the greenhouse there were tomato and cucumber plants, both still bearing fruit, and courgettes were still growing in the cold frames. The greenhouse was heated.

The party food was different: lots of assorted pickled salads, the smell of which will stay with me as an abiding memory! Raw cloves of garlic which we were invited to dip into salt, seems to be a delicacy. Then there was of course vodka! We were offered vodka with a difference, however, the one we tried had ginseng in it, they said it was good for your heart!!

Without doubt our most exciting adventure to date has been the helicopter flight out to the mine site. We were advised to wrap up warm as the locals were predicting snow on the ground. Stephen had a bet that there would be none. He won! It was cold, however, on account of the wind chill factor.

The flight was amazing, over eerie mountain ranges, scrubland and over the acid smelling mouth of a volcano which was gently smoking. Superb! Sadly, our digital video camera has chosen to break and we were only able to take still photos.

At the first mine site I was unable to go into the adit[2] as the Russians do not respect health and safety in the way we do, and as they had neglected hard hats Stephen would not allow me underground. So I had a wander around on surface, on my own, bear hunting (just joking, mother), and then waited in the helicopter, enjoying a snack of black bread and garlic sausage.

Next we flew to the hot springs and despite the zero temperature we went swimming. AMAZING! Hotter than a really hot bath, wouldn't like to say what an analysis of the water would reveal, but never the less a spectacular experience. I tried not to think about what I was walking on at the bottom of the water but concentrated on keeping afloat. I think it was probably the one and only time I've been swimming and was more concerned with keeping my feet off the bottom rather than being able to touch the bottom!

A good picnic lunch. Stephen was delighted with the smoked salmon. Then back onto the helicopter and on to the next site. Rodnikova. All these sites are in the middle of nowhere and can only be reached by air, which is probably the major challenge for the whole project. This time the adit was blocked but we had a look at where the gold ore had been dumped and could be processed at any time. Now, this site was apparently also a sort of ski tourist attraction. There were wooden chalets and a sauna. The

---

[2] Horizontal access to an underground mine.

area was built on hot springs which are used for heating. I'm not sure whether they were used to generate other power as well. We were offered some hospitality before we flew to the top of the mountain to look at another part of the site. Stephen wanted to investigate some technical aspect. Praise must be given to the helicopter crew. They were most professional and extremely skilled, landing on the top of mountains and ledges not much wider than the base of the helicopter. The weather conditions were not excellent as there were some very strong gusts of wind, plus the fact that they were flying between mountain ranges.

We did see some brown bears. There were two playing in a river as we flew over, sadly they were in the distance so we did not manage to get a good view of them. Never mind, there is always the next time!

Friday saw us working in the office, with Anglo-Russian relationships sorely tested through difficulties with technical data interpretations! When we got back to our hotel there was a wedding reception in full swing. It was good fun to watch, they were very organised and were playing loads of team games men versus women including, of course, downing vodka shots!

Some of Saturday was spent in the office but we also found time during the afternoon to explore the area close to our hotel. We found a book shop which was more of an educational stationers, selling text books, maps, maths equipment, paper etc. We bought some postcards, I think we'll venture back there again sometime. We were the objects of interest, I don't think they get many English people shopping there. Next we visited a local supermarket. It was small by our comparison but never the less well stocked and despite my doubts to the contrary, they do have Nescafe coffee, including Cap Colombie! Even more essential than that, they sold Cadbury's chocolate and Mars bars!!! Well stocked, we returned to the hotel for dinner and to watch a DVD.

Sunday was an uneventful day really because Stephen had a lot of work to do at the office. I went off during the day to look at a different hotel, we are still in search of somewhere quieter. The new hotel was fine except that it cost nearly three times as much as the current one because we are not Russian. They were prepared to negotiate the price if we stayed for more than a month. So now we are looking to see if we can rent an apartment. During the night there were more nocturnal activities, it cannot be healthy!!

And we still have the ongoing saga of the laundry! But I'll save that for another day, by which time it might be resolved. Bath and sink plugs do not come as standard in the hotel rooms in this country! This makes doing your own washing tricky. The thing is, last week, we had some washing done at the hotel and they charged £20. Their rates were rather high to say the least, so we tried to ask our office staff to help us negotiate with the hotel or find somebody else to do the laundry for us. It has taken five days but we now have Vera who will do our laundry for a fixed rate. She is a geologist who works across the corridor from Stephen. I'm a happy bunny now. You see it doesn't take much to keep me happy!

On Monday evening there was a birthday party at the hotel. As the guests arrived they brought flowers with them. Magnificent specimens, I don't know where they are grown but there is a whole row of about eight or nine kiosks selling flowers that we pass on our way to the office. They all have such long stems, some people brought one rose, or a single chrysanthemum, others a bunch of flowers and there was one plant. Although the partying went on long into the night and we could hear them singing, they didn't keep us awake. Our best night's sleep to date!

Life here is full of complex contrasts, human and environmental, a dichotomy of existence.

Tuesday dawns, another beautiful, crisp day, the volcano looks stunning as the sun shines down. It is the people that make up a country, the way they think, live and co-exist. This country is such a contradiction, it is so confusing, it is human nature to make comparisons but sometimes it is the wrong thing to do.

Next week: the people.

I'm sitting at a desk in one of the offices, I work here, sometimes on my own, while the others work down the corridor. Pasha, a geologist has just come in, he speaks no English and I no Russian, so we communicate in a very basic manner. He came in and switched on the lights and then bantered on about something in Russian, me nodding away, I could have been agreeing to anything, then in comes the interpreter to tell me that Pasha says we should keep the lights on all the time. It would seem that whether they are on or off we pay the same! Strange.

Carol's flight checks for the
ME8 helicopter flight.

Flying over the Mutnovskaya crater.

Landed and going for a swim!

Swimming in the hot springs,
air −15 °C, water +30 °C.

THE BED

Carol Lay

From:	Carol Lay
Sent:	27 October 2001 13:34
Subject:	Journeys 3 This weeks message to you all

JOURNEY WITH MY HUSBAND
PART 3

Petropavlovsk-Kamchatsky, Kamchatka
Thursday 25 October 2001

This is a very strange country to live in. Probably the biggest hurdle for us is the language barrier; you cannot pick up clues from tone of voice, speed of conversation or the spoken word itself. The pronunciation is complex and you have to tune in your listening skills to be able to hear the minute differences between some of the "e", "ch" and "C" sounds. As in English there are a series of standard phrases: for greetings; thanks; passing the time of day and such like. Stephen has several of these and I am getting better... slowly, very slowly! "медленно", pronounced "medelena".

Quite a few of the staff at the office speak English, two quite well and one passably. There are two interpreters who do a really good job, translation of the written as opposed to the spoken word is quite complex too, many of our words and terms do not translate easily into Russian and the same can be said of Russian to English. Where technical data is involved it is increasingly difficult.

However, it is possible to have conversations, and Stephen and I are getting better at using specific vocabulary instead of jargon. This week we had to explain what we meant when we said "pass" and what a "rain cheque" was. Then Sergei, who is our driver, wanted an explanation for the meaning of "motion" and "emotion" and where was the connection between the two? As for explaining "tricky"... we settled on "difficult"!

We have been out and about a bit more, exploring the city. Sergei took us to look out over the city on a road that will be unusable in a few weeks once the snow arrives. The views were incredible. Mountains and volcanoes as far as the eye can see. There is already fresh snow on top of the mountains and apparently, the deadline for the arrival of snow is November 5th! Every city has a Lovers Lane and Petropavlovsk is no different! We drove up Lovers Hill, there were about four wedding parties taking place. When we stopped to take photos there were a group of youths just messing around, who took an interest in us taking photos and for some reason thought we were Australian. We said "no, English" and that was like giving them an open invitation! Half the group was learning English at college and they wanted a chance to practise their linguistic skills. They were excellent, and we almost had to prise ourselves away from them after having the obligatory photos taken!

Our exploring took us out to the edge of the Pacific Ocean. Magnificent! There was a fair bit of surf rolling in and the sand was black as a result of the volcanic activity. We couldn't see Japan but we imagined it in the distance. We drove along a road that was beside the military area and on the opposite side there were several ancient military tanks parked and abandoned. They were positioned in readiness for sea defence against Japan etc. "Scary" as Nay (our daughter) would say!

The other morning Stephen said, "Do you realise we couldn't be further away from home than we are here!" Why he felt the need to tell me that I haven't quite fathomed because at the time I was wondering how the cockroaches who were not supposed to cross over the chalk lines[3] had decided it would be okay for them to do so?!

We had some snow this morning 23rd October. It was heavy and lasted for a couple of hours but soon thawed. Initial excitement was played down by Stephen who reminded me that once it really started it wouldn't stop for about six months, killjoy!

We're on the move, leaving the hotel and moving to an apartment. I went to look at it on Sunday: a bedroom; day room; kitchen and bathroom. The owner is on business in Vladivostock, so we are renting it until we come home in December. There was no bed, so Monday saw me with Sergei the driver looking for beds. Interesting experience! Apart from the fact that Sergei has limited English and I have even more limited Russian. When sign language, gesture and shoulder shrugging failed we rang the office to speak to Natasha, the secretary/interpreter, to answer the questions. In Petropavlovsk, like Moscow, all the calls within the city are free and dotted about the city there are telephone booths, very useful. Back to the bed. It appears that because of the limited room in apartments, most people purchase bed settees, however, as Stephen and I like a bit of

---

[3] A 'chalk' line of lime is drawn on the wooden floor around the skirting board and around the legs of the bed, chairs etc. Cockroaches, apparently, don't cross these lines!

comfort and have been sleeping on the bed from hell at the hotel, I was keen to buy a divan. A couple of phone calls later, Sergei had asked all the necessary questions and yes we could get a bed and have it delivered by the weekend. The furniture stores were reminiscent of the sixties early seventies, we went to four or five stores one of which was like a mini Courts[4], all the others sold a variety of furniture, plus electrical goods, general household paraphernalia, and second hand clothing and footwear. An interesting morning.

But, now we're not buying a bed, we are renting one, it is to be hired and delivered to our apartment by Thursday, when we plan to move in! We have hired Anna who will clean and do the laundry for us, and who will cook if we want her to. We are reserving judgement on that one until I've tried out the little cooker. We are desperate for some real food!!

There is so much to tell people about, all things to do with living right in the midst of a very different culture that has such a different history from our own, which is responsible to a greater or lesser extent for the way people live and behave now. The people, the way of life, the food, the cost of living, people's expectations and acceptance of their lot as if they have no way of changing the outcome.

Wherever you live, your country, your culture, is dependent on the people. People tend to fall into categories, types, and although it might be wrong to try and fit people into boxes it is human nature to do so. Here is no different, except that maybe you need a few extra sub-categories! So where to start?

There is no doubt that we have been in contact with those for whom the communist ideals are still very much alive and operating. People who get things done by intimidation, the speed with which they achieve goals is due to this "do as I say or expect the consequences" attitude. They feed off this power, and believe in it, inflicting fear and anxiety. Their country, they believe, has little or no need for Westerners, either their expertise or money! They create such heavy atmospheres wherever they are which is counterproductive to the creation of a team or joint working process, possibly because such a modus operandi could threaten their autonomy! It is a shame that an intelligent person should be entrenched in such ways of working, especially as this person exudes all the trappings of wealth… fine clothes, stays at expensive hotels, travels first class. It certainly makes Stephen's job so much more difficult, it is a sign of a good day's work when he takes one step forward and none backwards!

---

[4] UK retailer of furniture and electrical goods

Last night we were guests of the Rotary Club of Petropavlovsk. My Uncle Jack would have been very proud of us! The Club meets at the hotel we're staying at. Valentina, who is married to a person at the office, introduced us to the members and had arranged for an interpreter, although several people spoke excellent English. The Club consists of about 15 members, all of whom, except the treasurer, are women! We have our own ideas about this! They are a much poorer club than Camborne Rotary, and although they had the bell and gavel it was difficult to follow the proceedings. There were a group of youngsters there, we think they were Rotaract, who had been on exchange visits to America, and one chap who was on an exchange visit to Kamchatka from Brazil. It would seem that the club puts a lot of effort into raising money to support these exchanges. The youngsters, who spoke brilliant English, told us about their exchange experiences and one of the members said something like it was good to give young people the chance to pull themselves out of this swamp. There was an auction and Stephen bought some old paper money, a 1919 ten rouble note. After the meeting we chatted to the youngsters, Zoya told me my English accent was awesome! This was probably because she spoke English with a real American drawl! They were great fun and we are going back in a couple of weeks and Stephen is going to be their speaker, Stephen was presented with a banner to take back to Camborne. One of the members works at a local hospital so I am hoping that maybe she will take me there on a visit - she can speak English, having worked on an exchange in Australia.

Well, we still haven't moved into our apartment, there is a problem with the bed, maybe by next time we write......

EXPERTS

Carol Lay

From: Carol Lay
Sent: 08 November 2001 05:58
Subject: Journey Part 4

Dear All

Hope you are not too bored with hearing about our ventures. I am desperately hoping that by the next time I write I am going to be able to report snowfalls to you. In fact I'll probably be grumbling about them.

NEWSFLASH! IT'S SNOWING!!

Love Stephen and Carol

JOURNEY WITH MY HUSBAND
PART 4

Petropavlovsk-Kamchatsky, Kamchatka
Monday 29 October 2001

zdra-stooy-tye, this means "hi" in Russian! Here it is spelt phonetically, it is actually spelt like this: зДравствуйте, easy! This is the greeting most commonly used but even the Russians have problems with it and say "zdrast"! Another greeting is do-bra-ye-oo-tra or in Cyrillic, доброе утро (good morning). What happens at the office is they try to say "Good morning, Carol" and I have a go at "zdra-stooy-tye", I'm better at saying "do-bra-ye-oo-tra" though! It is the same in the evening, they have learnt to say "bye, bye, see you tomorrow" and we've learnt to say, "do svee-da-nee-ya" (до свидания). We also say "spa-see-bo" ("thank you", спасибо). So there, a little bit of Russian for you. I might share some more with you later!

Well, the big move took place last Friday. Hurrah! We now live at : Петропавловск-Камчатский, БуЛьвар РЫбацкой СлавЫ, Дом 3 кв 78! We have no idea what this says, except it's block 3 and apartment number 78! We have this typed out lots of times to show to taxi drivers in case we need to get home. I'm fibbing a bit, because the first part of the address says Petropavlovsk, and the next bit is Kamchtsky, it's after that we flounder!

And just as I thought I was beginning to hack the smells, guess what, on Friday there were two new ones. They were both connected with the move. Although the bed problem had not been fully solved, as the American fisherman with the bed was stuck at sea due to the weather, we were so desperate to move we decided to make do with a bed settee, so the move could take place! This decision came about suddenly as a result of another bad night's sleep, on account of the hotel's nocturnal activities plus being consistently overcharged. Eventually, enough is enough. Consequently, in the middle of Friday morning a cab arrived at the office to take Youri the interpreter, and me back to the hotel, to pack and move our chattels to the new abode!

Cue the first smell. The taxi… a mixture of bodies, vodka, and vomit, thankfully it was only about a fifteen minute journey, which cost 80 roubles[5] (рубль), about £2. Packed and paid up we left to drop off the luggage at the apartment, in a different taxi. Mission accomplished we returned to the office via three banks. Youri had to exchange some dollars for roubles for Stephen. Not a difficult task you may think, but it was. At the first place we stopped, they wouldn't exchange the money because they said it was counterfeit, well they were brand new notes, at the second place they had only enough roubles to be able to change part and so we ended up at the third 'bank'. You would never have found any of the banks on your own. But then none of the buildings appear to be shops or offices or anything in particular as they all have the same facade.

Anyway, back to the move. So the luggage was there, now we had to get the bed settee from the day room to the bedroom. Picture three men trying to get a rather large bed settee through a rather small archway, well two men really, Youri and Pacha, they insisted on doing the job without Stephen's help. However, they had to concede in the end to having help from the 'expert' (more of experts later). After about fifteen minutes of pushing and pulling the task was completed, exit Youri and Pacha, enter Anna, the lady who 'does'. Leaving Anna to make up the bed, with instructions to return "завтра, завтра, завтра", (zavtra, "tomorrow, tomorrow, tomorrow") because we didn't know what "Monday" in Russian was, Stephen and I set off to purchase some provisions for our evening meal. Now I have to say Stephen was not best pleased at this idea, as he thought I'd already done the shopping, I mean what was I doing all day? Whatever, he quickly got into the spirit of the exercise and we set

[5] In 2001 there were about 40 roubles to £1, or 1 rouble was worth about 2½ pence.

out. We looked and looked and looked. Eventually we found a department store where we could get enough for the night, they had coffee (кофе, "corfy"), bread (хлеб, "kleb"), cheese (сыр, "seyr"), pasta, ketchup, and yoghurts, orange juice and milk (молоко, "molako"), so we wouldn't starve! We got a bit of western 'attitude' from a young assistant too.

Back at the apartment...... we began to settle in. I could go on at length about the idiosyncrasies of the kettle, oven and electricity but I'll pass on these for a moment to tell you about the smell! The whole place has a smell, but the bathroom, can you guess, the drains are minging!! When people in the above apartment use their bathroom then it is humungus minging!! I don't think this translates into Russian very well. You really don't want to know anymore do you, suffice it to say, that it is unwise to be in our bathroom at the same time they use theirs. Sometimes, one learns extremely quickly from an experience, thank goodness!

Actually, bearing in mind where we are, the state of the country and its economy, we are in a good area, and in comparison, it is quite tastefully furnished and decorated, all things are relative. We are comfortable, we can please ourselves and the quality of food is better, most of the time, considering there is only one electric ring that is a bit temperamental!

Let me take you back to the experts. To do this I must introduce you to Micha. He is "a geologist by education", Stephen generally has high regard for geologists though this particular one is doing the profession no favours! He speaks little English, but I think he understands more than he admits. He sometimes drives us, and road rage cannot describe either his style of, or attitude towards, driving, we are always happier when it is Sergei driving.

Micha is an "expert". He knows everything there is to know about this gold deposit Stephen is working on. The "Westerners" know nothing; all they do is use their box of iron, commonly known as a computer. In the term "Westerners", he includes not just Stephen and the company but also a team of Australian consultants who are involved in the project and who have requested some answers from Micha. First big mistake. He is the expert, but he cannot answer the questions because he doesn't understand them, they mean nothing in Russian terms. This is a daily battle for Stephen.

It doesn't end there though. In the office they have a photocopier, it doesn't work, Stephen suggested somebody spent some time taking it apart and cleaning it... but no, we have to get the expert. He, the expert, is too busy, he cannot come, the expert says... do you get my drift? We have a Library, which is where I am based. The shelves are bursting with irreplaceable maps and documents. Stephen asked Micha for some fire extinguishers… "We have to ask the expert from the fire department, he is busy". Then there are the leads for the computer "… yes we need to ask the expert but he cannot come, his schedule is all booked up". And so it goes on. The man cannot or will not make a decision, he is too afraid, he will do nothing without somebody giving him permission. The man is unable to think for himself, you can imagine how difficult Stephen finds this sort of attitude to work with. He is a entrenched in a system where there is always somebody to tell you when to speak, to breath, to smoke and so on. People do not need to think for themselves. In the man's own words, there is an expert to do this. How can East meet West. Does East want to meet West? Can it be bothered to learn how to think for itself or would it rather just carry on the way it is? I would not even try to answer these questions, but it would seem that many would rather take the easy option, because to invoke change would almost cause a revolution. The psychology would have to do a huge U-turn and who can predict what the consequences might be? Much too deep for me.

Shall I move onto a lighter note and update you on the weather, volcanoes and earthquakes? Today it is minus 4 °C, there was a heavy frost and ice on the inside of some windows, but still no snow falling here. Yesterday felt colder because of the wind chill factor, it was −2 °C. I made a big mistake and wore a skirt - last night I packed it!

We can no longer see the volcanoes from our new apartment unless we lean right out, but we see them on our way to and from the office. They have more snow on them and one is still gently smoking. As for the earthquakes, funnily enough we haven't felt any since we left the hotel.

I want to tell you about going to the market. It was such a tremendous experience. We had such fun buying potatoes I'm worried we're losing it big time! Obviously, from the list I gave you earlier, we hadn't got enough food in the place to live on so we decided to go to the market; nothing like fresh fruit and veg is there? Quite, nothing like fresh fruit and veg…! Armed with a pretty long shopping list we headed off to explore and buy washing up liquid, pan scrubbers, fly spray, bleach, rubber gloves, disinfectant, air spray and food. Detergents more or less purchased we began to look for Tesco. Dream On! We found several shops and made a few purchases, Stephen was disgusted at having to pay 4 roubles, 10p for a carrier bag. Eventually, we reached the market. It was after midday, but shops don't open until 11 a.m. so they were only just getting going when we arrived.

Who needs to speak a foreign language when you've got a finger to point with? The potatoes were already weighed out in buckets sitting on the counter so we pointed at a bucket and had the contents poured into Stephen's priceless bag. Cinch! Next for the carrots, these were bagged up and priced, we just had to choose between a big or small bag. This done we moved onto buying some readymade cabbage salad. Now the fun began, much to the amusement of the stallholder and all the market people within hearing distance! We seemed to have suddenly grown two heads each! After much pointing and tasting of various salads; cabbage, carrot, beetroot, we settled on the cabbage one. "How many kilograms" she asked. "Nyet" (нет, no) we say and try to explain 500g or ½ kilo. She cottons on and we have to pay. Thank goodness for calculators, she keys in the amount and we pay. A successful transaction, we move along the rows of stalls, building up our stamina for the next purchases. And so it goes on, where they don't have calculators, they write down the amount, where this is not an option then they count out on their fingers. We knew we were the objects of interest from all the stares we were getting, but they were friendly and everybody did their best to help.

Probably one of our most abiding memories will be the meat market. I'm not really sure where to start. I suppose it was a room about the size of a country village hall. Around the sides were small stalls, selling meat, cooked sausage, sausages, and lumps of fat. In the centre there were men with axes chopping up huge carcasses and hacking away at lumps of frozen meat. Included was a man with only one arm, I dread to think what happened to the other one, perhaps a finger in too many pies?! This activity was surrounded on all sides by counters, again covered in meat, from frozen to thawing to fresh. So you had a mixture of butchers and sales people milling around together amidst, blood, guts, gore and chops. There was offal mixed in with everything else. Hearts, kidneys and huge slabs of liver. Some meat was cut like a joint, there was mince and there was diced meat. Some of it was ready bagged and only needed weighing. We bought some chicken pieces, three, I only wanted two, but there were three on the tray and I think the woman wanted to clear the tray, so we had them all, and we bought ½ kilo of mince. We wrote down 500g and she was fine. The label said 50 % something and 50 % something else! I think it was the meat/fat ratio. Still it only cost just over £2 for both. And it tasted okay, the chicken was better than the mince! In and amongst all of this were a huge amount of dogs looking for bones. This seemed to be quite normal! I have learnt that there are times here when I just have to close my eyes and pretend not to see some things.

One of these things was the woman in the grocery store near the apartment who cut off some smoked sausage for us. Her hands were the colour of… It's much better not to think about it! It is at this store that we bought a bottle of gin and tonic, like you can buy a bottle of cider, which we also bought. The G&T cost 65 roubles (£1.50) for 1½ litres was 9 % and quite drinkable. The cider made all the difference to the chicken stew!

I'll tell you about the tomatoes another day.

This morning we were sitting having breakfast when Stephen looked across to where we have a pile of tapes and DVDs. One is entitled 'Russian in 3 Months'. His comments were something like, perish the thought, better only stay 11 weeks!

And there is one more thing, Stephen and I are beginning to smell Russian, we'll need a good scrub and an airing on the washing line when we get back home!

To be continued……

VALUE OF MONEY
Carol Lay

From:	Carol Lay
Sent:	12 November 2001 06:54
Subject:	Journey with my Husband Part 5

Dear All

Here is the next instalment, I hope you will manage to find the time to read it! I forgot to mention that we are still on the sofa bed, but we are reasonably comfortable when we align ourselves between the metal bars! No snow today, just ice, ice and more ice, and still the women wear their high heeled boots!

Love to all

Stephen and Carol

JOURNEY WITH MY HUSBAND
PART 5

Petropavlovsk-Kamchatsky, Kamchatka
Monday 5 November 2001

Well the snow has arrived at last, lots of it: very wet, very fine and a lot falls at once! Last Friday evening saw us out walking with an American colleague to a restaurant which had been recommended by a chap in the office. We were well dressed for the weather, snow boots, hats, scarves and gloves and it was good fun. When we arrived at the restaurant, the Press Club (apparently it was once run by 'The Mob') we found a nice little place with about half a dozen tables, a bar in the corner and the menu all in Russian! The staff didn't speak any English, but fortunately, the Yank spoke almost fluent Russian so we were okay. We enjoyed a good meal and they sold real gin and tonic, so I enjoyed a couple (?) of those as well. The meal was comparatively cheap, about 8,000 roubles or £20 for three of us. A chap, on hearing our accents asked if he could join us to practise his English, we declined and later, when I was having a look around at people, you know: what were they wearing; who were they with; general people-watching, he asked me "am I boring"...... don't say a word, don't even go there!

On Saturday we were taken on a 'journey to hell' to the hot springs at

Paratunka. The hot springs were absolutely superb. There was an outdoor swimming pool in the middle of the woods. Beside the pool there was a building with the changing rooms, cloakrooms etc. So, you get changed indoors and then you go outside to the pool, where there are clouds of steam rising from the water, you can hear voices but you can't see people. It's useless for spectacle wearers, you have to wear your contact lenses or feel your way! Not very good for photos either. Anyway, you climb into the pool, it is about four times the size of our swimming pool at home, and it's like walking into a really hot bath. It's heated geothermally. At one end there was a smaller pool and that was even hotter, too hot to stay in unless you had just got out of the water and taken a walk in the snow which surrounded us. It was amazing, you're swimming around in this water with sweat dripping into your eyes and then up a few steps and you're in the snow in your swimming costume with bare feet just so you can cool down. We stayed in for about an hour and it was really relaxing. It cost 70 roubles (about £1.75). There are 40 roubles to the £ at the moment.

On the subject of money, in the cities all money-speak is in roubles or US Dollars. In the remote areas there is no interest in the $. To put the hardships of the normal Russian in perspective you must realise that it was less than 10 years ago that 1 rouble would buy £1. When Stephen was at Archangel in 1995/96 the rouble had devalued to about 4,000 roubles to £1. Since, they devalued the rouble so that there are about 3 roubles to the £1 and now we have an exchange rate of 40 roubles to the £1. So, £1,000 worth of roubles saved ten years ago is worth about £0.02p now! The range of currency in common usage is 1,000 rouble notes (£25) down to 1 kopek (100 to the rouble) = 1/100th of 2.5p!! This must be an indication of the spread between the poor and the rich.

About the journey. We were invited to make this trip by Youri's wife Valentina. She is very keen on spending time with foreigners and likes to speak English, which she does really well. Anyway, this trip was planned throughout the week and we were to go to the hot springs with Valentina and her friends as Youri had other business to do. Fine, they would pick us up from the apartment at 2 p.m. in their Japanese 4WD. Youri only has professional friends, and we were going to meet a dentist, the best in the city, and a gynaecologist. But in the end we met neither, as Olec took us and Youri came too. Olec imports cars from Japan and sells them somewhere and he was responsible for our "Journey from/to Hell". The roads were icy from the previous day's snowfall. He had just collected this Toyota saloon from the deck of a ship and I don't think he knew how to drive it. He drove on the wrong side of the road pretty much the whole time, with his foot touching the floor and total disregard for other road users. I seriously didn't think we were going to get back to Petropavlovsk in one piece, I don't think I have ever been so glad to get out of a car. Even Stephen was scared and kept muttering under his breath. Youri and Valentina seemed totally oblivious to our anxiety and Valentina chattered on in English asking us what we thought about Russian women, milk, bread and so on. This weekend we are going to her house for lunch. We are walking there!

We've been finding out about how much people earn and how much they need to survive each month. They reckon they need $400 a month to live, which is 12,000 roubles or £300. If they teach, or are in the medical profession and are paid by the government they earn about 1,900 roubles a month (yes the comma is in the right place!), if they are paid at all. They tell us they can go for up to six months without being paid and when we ask how they live at these times they just shrug their shoulders. We pay our cleaning lady $100 a month, we are her only source of income apparently so how does she survive? Our apartment is costing 2,500 roubles each month (£64), local phone calls are free, electricity and heating are about 100 roubles each per month (£2.50).

The cost of food is variable, depending on where you shop, obviously the market is cheaper, but then prices vary considerably from one supermarket to another. We found a very westernised supermarket last week, they pack your shopping and you get free carrier bags but only because you are paying 20 % to 80 % more for your shopping. There is a 'hole in the wall' there for money, it has English instructions but last time we used it it ran out of money! I did buy some Heinz baked beans for £0.80p last weekend and it is self-service which I liked, but reminded Stephen too much of Tesco! We have two grocery stores right beside the apartment, bread is good and costs about 10.50 roubles (£0.25), so is quite cheap, but they only make small loaves. Cucumbers were 45 roubles a kilo (£1.10) at the market and apples are 35 roubles a kilo. On the whole it must be a daily challenge to these people to live within their budget. Daily shopping must make it harder. We haven't really looked at and compared the prices of clothes and shoes yet as we've been too busy looking for food bargains in the market! They seem to eat a great deal of cabbage as well, mainly in salads, it probably takes too long to cook. Apparently, as well as the traditional borsch, there is also a traditional cabbage soup which we are having when we go out to lunch. They sell big plastic bags of biscuits for 17 roubles, they probably weigh 1 kilo. Last week I thought

CAROL LAY

I'd bought some gingernuts, only to find they were very well done flour and water! I bought some sort of thick morning-coffee type ones as well and they weren't up to much either. The week before we had coconut ones which were fine and we've had wafer ones in the office.

Sadly, coffee and gin are very costly! My favourite instant coffee is well over £6 here. It would be about £2.50 at home and gin is about three times the price it is at home, so I'll just have to wait because we have challenged ourselves to keep within a budget, not a severe Soviet one but not too western either! We had liver last night, 20 roubles, but the Lay crisps for starters and the special yoghurts pushed the budget up a bit, and don't tell Stephen but the grapes I bought cost 75 roubles! Well sometimes you just have to spoil yourselves, don't you!

Life in the office is never dull! This week I'll tell you a bit more about Youri. He is a bit of a Mr Fix It! He is originally from the Ukraine but has lived in Petropavlovsk for 20 years or more. He works here as an interpreter and logistics man and he located our apartment and Anna. Poor chap also gets the blame for anything that goes wrong there, specifically the telephone! He went to England in 1976 and talks about that a lot, it was quite something at that time to go to England and he says he was one of only about 300 from the whole of Russia do so. He has travelled widely, mainly I think as a fisherman; he obviously loved the travelling and is proud of what he has done and rightly so. His daughter, who lives in Chicago, works for the police department and is married to an American who is a policeman. The more I talk with Youri the more I feel for him. He is an intelligent man, who just cannot move forward because of circumstances here. He is extremely proud of having friends who are foreigners and talks about them endlessly.

His English is good, but his wife's is better as far as conversational English goes. He tells me he doesn't want to live here anymore because it is too tough, but that he cannot move anywhere else.

We haven't seen a great deal of the volcanoes this week as they've been hidden either by clouds or snow flurries, but when they have been apparent, they, and the mountains, are stunning. We went for a slippery walk last Sunday afternoon to see if we could find a short cut that we could walk to the office. We think we might have, but it is too icy to try at the moment, maybe this weekend. Anyway, while we were walking we came across what looked like a shanty town. A small community of wooden homes, more like shacks than houses. They seemed to have electricity, but because they all had chimneys and wood piles we came to the conclusion that they probably didn't have the central heating which is fed around the

26

city to all the apartments. These homes had small patches of garden attached to them, the soil was dug but we didn't see any plants, they were probably all harvested and either pickled or hung to dry, being stored for winter. There were quite a few animals as well: lots of extremely furry cats and chained up noisy dogs. There are lots of dogs around, even people in our block of apartments have dogs and some of them are great wolf sized hounds. I suppose they have to be to keep their tummies and bits off the snow, very chilly thought!

And so I come back to the snow. There is no way Cornwall would cope with this snow! Having said that, last week I saw the tyre people doing a marvellous trade in winter tyres. You would expect that in a country where snow is the norm and it always snows by November 5th, that they would be prepared, but no, this is Russia, and they wait for the snow and the ice and the accidents and then they get their winter tyres out of hibernation. They are some tyres too. They don't have spikes in them but the tread is amazing. I'm glad I don't have to drive on these roads in these icy conditions (I find it hard enough to walk!). After a snow fall it warms up a bit, just enough for a slight thaw and then it freezes again, so you have layers of ice, and if the wind blows as well you have some pretty patterns. Stephen has instructed me to walk away from the edges of the buildings because he doesn't want me to be stabbed by the falling stalagmites! Or is it stalactites? They take the snow for granted here, they don't even build snowmen! I think Stephen and I will have a go!

For those of you who haven't heard from our children, they are all well, Nay is having her usual dramas, but in French! She has got several part time jobs, teaching English and looking after children. Paris will never be the same again! Tam thinks studying is wonderful and is still deciding between medicine and clinical psychology for her doctorate, in between working shifts for a catering company. Ian has moved house and got parts in three productions: two main and one minor. He has had an interview for a job, but we haven't heard whether he was successful. Poppydog, we understand, is much happier now she has received her Frontline treatment for fleas although she still hasn't emailed us!

Well, I think that is about it for this week folks, except to recommend the film "Barber of Siberia" to you, it's a Russian film with a Hollywood Oscar, runs for about 3 hours, is in English and is jolly good.

No new smells to speak of and no quakes, however, more snow is forecast, next weather update to follow shortly......

THE FOX HOLE
Carol Lay

From:	Carol Lay
Sent:	18 November 2001 12:40
Subject:	Journey with my Husband Part 6

JOURNEY WITH MY HUSBAND
PART 6

Petropavlovsk-Kamchatsky, Kamchatka
Monday 12 November 2001

We had a super weekend with more little adventures and further insight
of life the Russian way! We got off to a good start on Friday evening when
Marc the Irish geologist on the project came back with us for dinner. We
slid our way to a supermarket recommended for its selection of wines and
safely carried home two bottles of South African wine. On our way there,
as we were manoeuvring the more icy parts of the path, a young man
interrupted our conversation most politely to ask us what we were doing
in Petropavlovsk and why we were out walking? He said he was
"bemused" by our answers, we told him we were living here and were on
our way to buy some provisions. As we parted from him at the traffic
lights he went off shaking his head in bewilderment!

Saturday morning saw us in the office first thing, I played on the
internet, doing some pretend 'retail therapy', whilst Stephen went for a
meeting at the Institute of Volcanics. Here he found out that cracks are
appearing in the Avacha volcano, the one that gently smoulders, and
people from the institute have to inspect it quite regularly. It looks as if
they are expecting an eruption anytime in the next hundred years! So watch
this space[6]!

After lunch our American friend came to see if we wanted to go out
and play! Together we slid down the road to the bus stop to catch a bus
to Yelizovo, some 25 km out of town and where the airport is. We missed

---

[6] Since Carol wrote this there have been several eruptions on Kamchatka,
including four concurrently in 2012/13.

the first bus because it was too full, so we got onto a Number 1, which took us to the 10th Kilometre. PK is a long city and stop-offs are measured in kilometres from Lenin's statue down town. The bus was about thirty years old, any of you who remember Grenville buses[7] will know the sort of thing I mean! You got on and off at the middle of the vehicle and fought your way up or down as you saw a space. There was a lady standing beside the door waiting to take your fare, which was 5 roubles (12½p), and give you a ticket. We had to confuse the issue didn't we? Stephen had got one 5 rouble coin out and handed it to her whilst he fiddled for another, in the meantime Marc had paid for two, but this has confused the woman who wanted more. Our American friend explained to her what had happened, but she was not convinced and spent the remainder of the journey telling him that if she had too much money or too little money she would be thrown into jail! At least we think that was the gist of it. There are seats on the bus, but it gets really packed, I'm reliably informed that people do not walk in Petropavlovsk, they always catch a bus or go by car. It was amusing to see the stares we got from fellow passengers when they listened to us talking. There are probably only about twenty English speaking foreigners in the city.

At the 10th kilometre we catch up with the bus we missed earlier but it is still too full. We wait in a very comfortable and sunny −3 °C and in rolls a mini bus or "routebus". This will also take us where we want to go but instead of costing us 10 roubles each it will be 15. We climb in! The driver thought he was at Silverstone. If anything had happened nobody would have stood a hope in hell. Perhaps this is an acceptable way to drive in icy conditions in this country. Who are we to argue, we've only been here six weeks!

We arrived unscathed, if a little stiff from the cramped seating and slowly slid through the streets of Yelizovo to the Fox Burrow Restaurant (the name is in English!), the reason for our outing. It was situated right next to the public banya (sauna), which is a regular haunt of families with no facilities in their apartments. Yelizovo is inland so it's a lot colder. The restaurant was lovely. We went into the bar to eat but there were a couple of others rooms as well. We were the only ones there to begin with so it was smoke free, an added benefit. The menu was good, lots of fish and seafood, and some traditional dishes. They didn't have any nuts but we had dried calamari to nibble on whilst waiting for our food. A couple of hours later, replete and relaxed, we made our way back to the bus stop.

---

[7] A bus company in Cornwall.

Our return journey was on a coach, far more sedate and very interesting for people watching. Fur coats and hats everywhere, like they were going out of fashion.

Sunday dawned and we had a lunch invitation from Youri at the office. I don't think Stephen's office is the best example of Russian friendliness, but this particular couple have tried to sell their country to us as being somewhere good to be! As we didn't know the way to their apartment, Youri came to fetch us, on foot. My God was it slippery! What made it seem worse was that it was a really beautiful, crisp day, the sun was shining, the sky was cloudless, and the sun shone on the ice and it glistened, and it said "try me and slide" ......! So I did, and I did, but not very much, I walked so slowly, that Stephen disowned me, he kept saying, "just walk, Carol, and don't think about it"! Of course I did exactly what was asked of me.

It took us about 35 minutes to get there. They live in a five year old apartment block, on the fifth floor and the views were astounding: out to the Pacific; mountains and volcanoes, fantastic. Their apartment was light and airy, sparsely furnished by our standards, but nevertheless it looked good. The entrance to the apartment and the stairs were in disrepair; it was difficult to believe it was only five years old. Graffiti on the walls, some written in English, paint hanging off, generally dank and miserable, but good compared with others we have seen. Tenants or owners pay a maintenance fee but they see nothing for it. There is no lift. The Soviet policy is that if there are less than six floors, you can manage the stairs, six or over and there is a lift! I don't know where the elderly and infirm live but I can't imagine climbing all those stairs with your arthritis or even a broken ankle.

We were made most welcome and lunch was excellent, some traditional Russian fare, cabbage soup, cabbage salad, meat and potato salad, fish from the market and then some pasty[8] shaped pastries which had fresh cranberries in them. I kept being asked, "Carol, you no like, why you not have more?"! All very delicious, but we have become used to eating far less than at home, and feeling better for it!

After lunch we chatted and exchanged information about our families, sharing photo albums and we also learnt a bit more about the Russian way of life, things they have learnt to accept. Valentina wanted to know why we had such a big house, why did we need so much space, what did we do with it all? If we had such a big garden why didn't we grow potatoes,

---

[8] Cornish pasty, well known throughout the world.

SMILE AND ENJOY THE ADVENTURE

everybody in Petropavlovsk has their own potato patch in case things get tough and they don't get paid!

We heard how western companies come to Kamchatka, set up businesses, employ masses of people, pay well, and then 'the system' kicks in: causing problems; changing legislation; rules; and so on, so the companies just up and leave, jobs go, no money. Sometimes the companies even leave all their assets, just cut their losses and get out. They cannot be bothered with the battle and take their money somewhere else. Who is the loser?

Valentina wanted to know where we eat in the evenings and we explained that I cooked. She was amazed! Then she asked if I cooked when we were at home. Again I said yes. Apparently she rarely cooks because it takes so long, and there I was thinking it was just the electric ring in our apartment that takes forever! But no. Marc, who has moved into an apartment has the same problem. He said he thinks the problem is that everybody is using the power at the same time. I said "yes, it's the same in Wendron[9] in an evening but it doesn't take half an hour to boil a kettle". He looked at me very patronisingly. He is far more sympathetic than I. I find it difficult to understand why they tolerate so much hardship, and wonder for how much longer things will remain the same.

Our walk back to the apartment was uneventful but unforgettable, as we walked the volcanoes turned from white to pink to yellowish as the sun set. Wisps of cloud hung around the summits as Avacha gently smouldered into the sky leaving a horizontal light grey line above the landscape towards the Pacific. Spectacular!

The snow and winter certainly seems to have settled in this week, with temperatures down to $-5\ ^\circ$C, but we haven't felt cold. You feel the chill when the wind blows. The apartment if anything is too hot, there are no thermostats, you can open the windows to cool down and that's it. The snow looks really pretty especially when it coats the branches of the trees, but when it freezes and re-freezes that's when the trouble sets in. There seems to be some sort of strategy to grit the main roads, but it doesn't seem to be done routinely, sort of when they remember. The main road is kept quite clear but there appears to be little thought to making things safe for pedestrians. "Where there is blame there is a claim" would have a field day here!

We were given two interesting pieces of information about travelling

---

[9] Carol's home village – it has a church, two farms, pub and a few houses. Her humour!

in these conditions either by foot or car! The first was, that if somebody offered to drive you in these conditions, they took responsibility for you...... some consolation I suppose when you are injured or worse! The second was that nobody cares here if you fall on the ice and hurt yourself, it is just tough, "so what", you fall......

Travelling home the other evening we hit a patch of ice which sent us sliding, Stephen and I already had our seat belts on, Marc reached to put his on only to be told by the driver, "don't worry, perfectly safe, I take responsibility for you!" They don't believe in car insurance either, it's too expensive. If you are found to be responsible for an accident, you have to take the damaged car and have it repaired, then return it to the owners!

You see, this is what I am struggling to understand, perhaps you can make some sense of it. You cannot select your own bag of frozen peas in the grocery shop, they are locked in the freezer cabinet in case somebody shoplifts, but you give somebody your car and car keys and trust them to return the repaired car to you.

This trust thing is weird, when we arrived here and collected our luggage we had to show them the baggage tickets we had been given in Moscow before we could take our luggage out of the hut. Where else would you do that?

Marc goes to the local gym here and he says there are about four different checkpoints to go through before he actually arrives in the gym. Shoe, check; bag, check; kit, check; literally as there is a "big, fat Russian mamma" watching the men change in the changing room, before they enter the gym. He reckons she's seen more dongs than smoked sausages! He pays about £2 to use the gym. Stephen says at least its keeping people in a job. I don't know.

They know how to dress for the cold here and believe fur coats are wonderful, what reason is there for bears, nobody needs them, they don't do any good, so kill them, it's no big deal and then you have a good coat or hat and you are warm! Any sort of hat goes, furry, woolly, with a bobble, but certainly furry is best and if possible it should look like sable! We stick to our fleece and woolly hats, although Stephen does have a synthetic fur one we may have to resort to. The women, or most of them, are still balancing in their high heels! I don't know how they do it. I have seen a few sliding around but it is an incredible balancing act. I think I'll stick to my big boots.

We are off to meet some English speaking people tonight. We were given their number and it turns out they live in the same apartment block as us, on the next floor. Rumour has it they make 'real' coffee. Here's hoping!

I think you ought to have an update on the job here. It's gruelling. There are daily disputes, which rumble on and remain unsolved. Some days I am up and down like a yo-yo as I always leave the room when there is an argument taking place. I fear some of the differences in culture, knowledge, experience and expectation are going to put a severe strain on what could be a really exciting venture. We know for certain that "there is gold in them there hills", but extracting it is going to be far worse than pulling teeth.

It is the differences between the cultures that make it really hard to adjust. It is exciting to be a part of it, even if you really are on the periphery, remember you have to live in Cornwall for about thirty years before you can be considered a local. In Petropavlovsk, I'm not sure you'd ever be fully accepted!

Don't get the wrong idea, we've met lots of people when we've been out and about who have been so friendly and helpful. At the market, in the restaurants, out walking and in our local shop they now say "hello" to us rather than a Russian greeting, we have tried hard to learn some of their vocabulary and it has been a give and take process.

But, ultimately, we are here for Stephen to do a job and it would seem that The Road to Asacha (where the gold project is, not the volcano Avacha) is going to be long and arduous and may be a bit like the road to Tipperary, but we'll just keep travelling on.

I sincerely hope we can make a go of this project. Before the summer people were working together, but if you remember the person I introduced you to in an earlier Journal you may understand where some of the difficulties stem from. The Soviet system has changed politically in some respects, but possibly not enough yet for Westerners to be able to work in partnership. This project is less likely to succeed if there is no mutual understanding and cooperation. The deposit can be the best ever, but if the will to succeed does not prevail we may as well face all the natural hazards that abound in Kamchatka, from avalanche to seismic events, volcanic eruptions and tsunamis, because that's how difficult the situation is.

The bed still hasn't arrived, I think it was lost at sea! We had a power cut last night but by the time we'd lit the candle it was back on. And the switch to the electric cooker ring is playing up...... it could be bread and smoked sausage washed down with G&T from now until we leave for home.

Oh yes, and the phone, have I mentioned the phone? It only works sometimes, we now find out that it is a party line, so if the people upstairs are using the line we can't, we are assured they cannot listen in to our conversations but that's not what I'd heard about party lines...... more soon!

The frozen Pacific coast just south of Petropavlovsk.

MEAT AND TWO VEG
Carol Lay

From:	Carol Lay
Sent:	25 November 2001 08:25
Subject:	Journey with my Husband Part 7

JOURNEY WITH MY HUSBAND
PART 7

Petropavlovsk-Kamchatsky, Kamchaka
Monday 19 November 2001

There are very few "Brits" here (well, only us and one other), we feel like intrepid explorers sometimes! However, the history of exploration in Petropavlovsk began many hundreds of years before we arrived!

1665: Kamchatka first appeared on a map drawn by Semion Remisov.

1697: Kamchatka becomes Russian territory, after an expedition led by Vladimir Atlasov

1697-1711: First settlements built by the Cossacks

1725-1730: The first Kamchatkan expedition is organised. Peter the Great and the Russian government were interested in finding a new land in the Far East and a strait between Asia and America. Vitus Bering led the expedition when the strait was found and named after him

1733-1743: During the second Kamchatkan expedition Petropavlovsk-Kamchatsky was founded on 17th October 1740. It was named after Bering's two ships: "Saint Peter" and "Saint Paul".

1741: Bering died on an island not far from Kamchatka, named Bering Island in his memory

1774: Captain James Cook's expedition visited PK. Later his assistant, Charles Clark (who recovered Cook's body) was buried here. He got sick at sea and died. Before his death he asked to be buried "in this wonderful land" which is what he thought about Kamchatka. A memorial to him is situated in the middle of town.

1860: Vladivostok was founded, altering the status of PK as Vladivostok became the centre of Russia's Far East as its location was far more suitable, for developing trade.

1868: The Russian government sold Alaska to the United States.

20th century: Kamchatka's destiny changed. It was largely forgotten from the late nineteenth century until the early part of the twentieth century. When the Soviet Government came to power, Kamchatka began to develop again. However, the peninsula was closed to foreigners and even Russians needed a special permit, so people could not appreciate either its beauty or its worth.

1992: Kamchatka is officially 'opened'.

21st century: British TV influence is felt. "Who Wants to be a Millionaire"; "Weakest Link"; "Wheel of Fortune"; "Paradise Island", "Breakfast TV"; all with identical sets and look-alike Chris Tarrants and Anne Robinsons; even a very realistic looking Barrymore interviewing children.

We met the one other English person last week. She originates from Somerset and is married to an American from Alaska. They have been living in Petropavlovsk for 10 years, having entered the country unofficially (with the blessing of the autocratic local Administration) before it was 'officially' opened to Russians and foreigners! When the area did open up and they officially applied for visas some very interesting dialogues with Moscow resulted! He speaks no Russian and she has some vocabulary and uses odd words, but cannot hold a conversation in Russian. They both teach English, she also gives talks about England.

At their home (next door!) we also met a couple of Russian women who are English teachers: one at a secondary school here in the city and the other teaches secondary children out in the country, about 150 km from here (where the temperature drops to −45 °C!). Their English was reasonable, though broken, and their spoken was much better than their comprehension. One was very reluctant to speak to us at all, she kept blushing and giggling. They earn $90 (£55) a month for 72 hours teaching! We were asked about discipline and corporal punishment in English schools as they had read that hitting children in schools was common! The teachers had only been learning English themselves for four years! They do well considering they actually have no exposure to true English speakers. Their ambition is to come to England and meet English people because they are "so polite"! All things are relative I suppose!

Although we were hoping for proper coffee we didn't get any but the tea, (чай, chay) was good and we shared some interesting marshmallow cake! They also lent us a Union Jack flag.

The English/American couple were very interesting; their main task in

Petropavlovsk is as missionaries for the Bahai faith. They spoke very little about this, other than to tell us this was the reason for their presence, and that they were kept very busy.

I asked the Russian English teachers where the schools were for the "brain damaged" children. They weren't sure, they knew of some orphanages, which I'd already been told about, but it would seem that handicapped children, if they are allowed to live, are probably kept at home! I have only seen one person in a wheelchair and one person who possibly had cerebral palsy in the two months we've been here. It does make you wonder! Mind you, pushing a wheelchair through the snow and on ice would be no easy task.

On these lines, we were watching the national news the other evening and they had a report from Vladivostok. It seems that they have adapted a bus to take wheelchairs. They showed a film of about five or six elderly disabled and wheelchair bound people going up two ramps, one balanced on the other, to get into a bus. There they sat in their chairs. No clamping in! Their escorts travelled with them, but had no seats, so stood holding hanging straps to keep their balance. In one sense it is a positive step, at least these people could travel, but yet again, health and safety didn't seem to focus in the planning. The angle of the ramps meant that two people had to push the chairs. Not a hydraulic lift in sight. It's a start. We don't always realise how fortunate we are in England.

Having received so many emails from you remarking on our visit to the meat market we decided we ought to go again in case we'd exaggerated the conditions. So, to confirm the truth we set off. We did the easy bit first and went to our regular vegetable stall, bought some different cabbage salad to try this week, it had peas and beetroot and raisins in, and a very peppery carrot, then we were ready for the meat market. We hadn't been exaggerating, it was just as we had described it! Dogs everywhere, entrails hanging over the edges of the tables, people wiping their nose on the back of their hands, it's a cultural thing you know, I won't go on...... On examination and after making a couple of circuits of the counters, we decided where we thought it would be safer to purchase some meat. We went for the chicken joints again, frozen from Florida apparently, and then we decided to buy some pork chops. Making ourselves understood by pointing and sticking up two fingers and saying "dvye" (две, two), the woman picked up the pile of chops, still semi-frozen, and carried them over to the axe man who proceeded to 'chop' off two from the pile while the woman held them steady for him! Now we know why they're called chops! They tasted okay and had no extra appendages with them!

Later in the day we headed for down town. It was a beautiful day, a bit cold but dry and sunny. So, well togged out, including woolly hats, we set off. It was still a bit icy underfoot but as long as you took small steps you were okay. I've come to the conclusion that as long as you walk as if you're flat footed and don't use your toes as you lift your foot, then generally you keep firm footed and don't slide too much.

It was about 6 km return walk and all uphill on the way back. Down town there is a huge market. Excellent for people watching. There were all sorts of stalls selling fur hats of every shape, size and hue, difficult to tell which animals they had originated from. And bobbles are definitely 'in' this year, on hats and coats! There were fur coats for sale and leather ones, costing anything from £500 to £1,000, which in itself is interesting because we keep being told how poor people are here. The cost of living is high, the wages are low, and yet there were plenty of people spending money. The people seem to choose to spend their money on clothes, make up, and hair-dos rather than food. A lot of beer and vodka is sold too and is remarkably cheap.

There was a fish market, really interesting, masses of fish, either salted, smoked or frozen, buckets of caviar in varying degrees of red and orange and different sized lumps, 600 roubles (£15) a kilogram, cheaper than fillet steak! There were some small plastic bags that had salmon trimmings in, enough to make a quiche or fish pie, (if you had an oven and not just a single electric ring, not that I'm complaining of course), and costing 12 roubles (30p)!

Eventually we found Covent Garden, Smithfield and Billingsgate all rolled into one! Flowers, fish and meat! More meat, but this time it seemed to be fresh and it looked much better, the steak looked as though it would be edible and I think that when we return in the New Year we will give it a try. Those serving even wore overalls and hats! It wasn't as exciting as the other one, but you can't have everything!

Our mission for Sunday was to visit the memorial to Captain Clark. We decided to walk, although there were a few flurries of snow fluttering around. This time it was about 6 km walk to get to our destination. A lovely walk which took us past down town and on past the statue of Lenin and along the seashore. Walking along the seashore it looked as if there was oil floating on the surface of the water, on closer inspection it turned out to be slushy ice. We couldn't decide whether the sea was beginning to freeze or whether bits of snow had been washed from the edge of the shore. On we walked until at last we found the monument. A single obelisk, standing about ten feet high, bearing an inscription to Clark. A square meter of British sanctuary ceded to England in the early 1900's! We posed beside it holding the Union Jack!

We decided to be brave and catch a bus part of the way back, and were well chuffed with ourselves when we managed to not only catch a bus and pay properly this time, but it was also going in the direction we wanted! After all the exercise we stopped off at the Avacha Hotel for some coffee. We ended up having lunch, the waitress recognised Stephen from when he had stayed before. She seemed very good at selling her wares! So we had Kamchatsky Soup, which had a bit of all sorts in but was good and hot, followed by pancakes with honey all washed down with coffee, for the magnificent cost of 179 roubles, just under £4.50. Rested we set off for home back up the long, long hill.

The week seems to have flown by and we have booked our tickets to fly back to Moscow for next Tuesday, 27th November, as long as it isn't snowing or there isn't a hurricane. Then we fly back to Heathrow on either Thursday or Friday.

We've had more snow this week, on Wednesday it was so bad we had to go home early from the office, and we thought that only happened in Cornwall, but like Cornwall it had stopped snowing by the time we got home. We made the most of the daylight and went out for a walk, feeling much more confident walking on snow, only to slip down! I slipped first, closely followed by Stephen. There was some sheet ice just sitting in wait under the new snow! The shopping bag split and we had to dry the soggy bread on the radiator! No harm done except to Stephen's pride, it was my second fall, so I'd already got over the pride bit! It is getting colder now, the communal thermometer outside the market reporting as low as −9 °C, which is not too bad until the wind blows which takes it down to below −20 °C with the wind chill factor. Brrrr.

Toddlers are pulled on sleds steered by their parents, it looks like lots of fun, but I think the children should wear crash helmets; I've told you how they drive around here!

Now here is something to ponder. At all the shops they give you a till receipt, but before handing it over they fold it and tear it! Why?

Well it's time to sign off for now, it's our turn to get the lunch and we've just discovered Petropavlovsk's answer to sausage rolls, it's surprising what you'll eat when you're hungry!

For those of you who are interested, the bed never did arrive, and we've had a few problems with the duvets which have caused some sleepless nights, so we thought we'd remedy the problem with some

Nytol[10], unfortunately we had the non-drowsy variety!

A little bit of family news, Ian has a part time job in a pub, on a month's trial, and Poppydog has her own email address, if you would like to email her, on Poppydoglay@hotmail.com. She was feeling left out! I'm not sure who pawt her up to it!

We know it's time to leave, we don't notice the smells anymore......

One square metre of Russia ceded to England.
The memorial to Charles Clark.

---

[10] "The UK's best sleeping tablet. A clinically proven night-time sleep aid helping you achieve a better night's sleep"!

VIP

Carol Lay

From:	Carol Lay
Sent:	03 December 2001 01:43
Subject:	Journey with my Husband Part 8

Dear All

Here is the last part for now. We arrived home safely and are now enjoying sleeping in a proper bed! Thanks for all your good wishes, we hope to catch up with you over the next few weeks.

All the best

Stephen and Carol

JOURNEY WITH MY HUSBAND
PART 8

Petropavlovsk-Kamchatsky and Cornwall, England
Wednesday 28 November 2001

Going out for a drink took on a whole new perspective the other evening when we stood under a clear starlit sky, ankle deep in snow outside a beer (пиво, pivo) kiosk, drinking half litres of beer, not me I hasten to add, I just kept Stephen and our American friend company! It was a memorable occasion. We'd met up with Rick earlier at his hotel, he is returning to the USA this weekend, his work in PK completed and realising we may not meet up again for some time we thought we'd have a get together. We shared a Korean meal before we walked back to our apartment, stopping on the way for the aforementioned beer! Rick used to live in an apartment across the road from where ours is, so he knows the area well. He took us up through the woods, which proved to be eventful as we were on ice a lot of the time!

I'm not quite sure what Rick's job is but he's a very interesting and knowledgeable chap. He speaks fluent Russian and was head hunted for his job for this skill. He was talking to us about the analemma. Brownie point for anybody who knows what this is and where you might find it. I'll give you a clue, we were talking about it in connection with our journey home and whether it would get dark as we flew north of the Arctic Circle!

He also informed us that last Sunday was Mother's Day in Russia. We didn't see many Mothers celebrating however.

Last weekend we went for our final visit to the market, we were disappointed that our vegetable lady was not there and there was somebody different on her patch. However, she was selling salads so we bought a beetroot one, only to find when we got home that we had bought ½ kg of raw grated beetroot! We had a couple of bits and pieces to buy as well but we gave the meat market a miss! This week we bought some smoked salmon to bring home, we had to wash the packets when we got back to the apartment to get rid of as much of the fishy smell as possible to make them packable! Well wrapped in several plastic carrier bags and then in cardboard to make doubly sure, they were ready for the homeward journey!

We visited our Anglo-American friends from next door at the weekend and this time we had some 'proper' coffee. The smell was wonderful! They are a well-travelled couple whose working lives led them to live in some extreme places with Sioux Indians, Navaho Indians and Eskimos and now in Petropavlovsk! Stephen was a bit outnumbered in a room with three teachers, we talked about education and the education system, and I think they will help me find a way into the schools when we return in the New Year. They were also telling us about working in cultures with completely different value systems and teaching people to respect the way others behave.

We've had an excellent time in Kamchatka, not always easy, but nevertheless interesting and exciting. It is difficult to understand some of the psychology of the people we were living amongst, their acceptance of living in a society which displays so little regard for fellow human beings, acceptance of the way things are and that there is no route to change. It is strange, they appear to care little for personal space. I first noticed this when we arrived in Moscow and I was waiting in a queue at the post office. There were two or three people in front of me, I thought two of them were together as they were standing so close together, one looking over the other's shoulder. It wasn't until the first person moved away that I realised they weren't together. They stand in the same sort of way when using the public telephones. Their manners are displayed differently from ours as well. Open a door and walk through it, steer a course on the pavement and keep going, no matter who is in the way. And then on the other hand, they talk to one another in great detail, whether they know them or not. They give personal information to complete strangers and everybody knows exactly what the other person earns, no secrets there!

Monday saw me slaving over a photocopier for most of the day, preparing endless documents for Stephen to bring home to work on. I was happily photocopying away and singing 'Frosty the Snowman' when to my horror a rat shot up through the floorboards and dashed across the floor, I shot in the opposite direction, shrieking until I reached the sanctuary of a chair, which I stood on! It wasn't spotted again that day and Stephen left strict instructions for it to be caught before our return! The library houses some irreplaceable documents, and the rat looked large enough to do some very serious damage if it wanted to!

Packing was interesting! Trying to fit everything in and be able to close the suitcases was a mammoth task, but eventually everything fitted and the lids were closed, locked and strapped. We were ready for home!

Aeroflot flights are not my most favourite things. I know it is probably illogical of me to be nervous of flying Aeroflot, they are probably as reliable as most others, but somehow they don't instil much confidence. We arrived at the airport and were ready to check-in only to be informed that the flight hadn't landed yet and check-in wouldn't be open for another ¾ hour. So we waited, surrounded by fur coats and fur hats. As people arrived they took their luggage to be 'wrapped up' in brown paper, securing them for the journey. On our outward flight from Moscow, fellow travellers had their luggage shrink wrapped by a special machine, whilst others who either couldn't afford the cost or had other things to spend their money on, secured their bags with Sellotape wrapped round and round!

When we checked in we had our translator to help us through. We paid extra to use the VIP lounge, which meant that when you checked in you told them which seats you would like, they write it down and take your tickets from you, plus payment for using the VIP lounge. Then they have to liaise with the other lounge by leaving the building we were in and walking next door where everybody else was checking in, to secure your seats before returning your tickets to you.

Now before you start to think we were in the VIP lounge because we are so used to BA lounges that we can't sit in the ordinary departure lounge any more, it is just a tad more complicated than that. In the other building there are no toilets! Plain and simple, and if any of you have ever travelled Aeroflot, you will understand why you need to use the bathroom before you fly! The other perk of using the lounge was that you got bussed to the plane rather than having to walk across the runway! The other interesting point was that our luggage was significantly over the allowance, about 25 kg which is charged at 90 roubles per kg. But by using the VIP lounge the total charged was significantly less than we were expecting! Draw your own conclusions!

Thankfully the flight was uneventful, but tedious, luckily I had saved "The Philosopher's Stone" to read which kept me entertained. The flight was delayed by 1½ hours and we waited on the tarmac for an hour of that time. They do an incredible job clearing the snow and ice from the runway. It was an amazing sight as we took off and flew away from the city and towards Siberia. Memorable and indescribable! I definitely want to go back.

Arriving in Moscow, nine hours later, it was snowing and seemed much colder than PK. We collected our luggage eventually from the carousel and struggled towards customs, having had the labels checked to ensure we hadn't taken anybody else's by mistake! They do not believe in trolleys at Moscow, so between us we carried and pulled six pieces of luggage and my handbag. At customs there was another security check, however if you had a porter with a trolley then all your baggage bypasses the security check! The security check was not there on Stephen's last visit, which suggests it has been introduced since Twin Towers, but as with many things in Russia, it is 'playing' at conformity, whilst still doing things their way!

It took us over an hour to reach our hotel and eventually we checked in. We needed to keep awake, because Moscow was nine hours behind Petropavlovsk, so we had been up a long time but needed to try and stay up for another few hours to try and help our body clocks adjust. We went in search of a cappuccino, followed by Kentucky Fried Chicken. Excellent! We kept going until about 8:30.

We were able to solve last week's enigma of why shop receipts are invariably torn. In communist times, and still practiced in many shops, the process of paying for your goods involves going to a central paying point to pay before taking possession of your goods. One takes the till receipt back to the counter and then take possession of your goods, the receipt is then torn to indicate that you have received what you paid for.

The hotel has two lifts. One of them creaks and drops a few inches when you get in it. So I practised my James Bond impersonation by getting my feet up on the side in case the bottom falls out! You may think she's really lost it now, but just wait until I tell you the next bit. On the day we returned home we had to do the courtesy bit of me visiting the people Stephen works with in Moscow. We arrived at the building and had to show our passports. But they wouldn't let us enter because there was no pass waiting for us. The man we were with dashed off to the office to get us one and ten minutes later we were making our way to the lift. The office was on the fifth floor, and the lift got stuck! Why? Because there were too many people in it! How did we get out? We had to bang against the sides, but that didn't work, so after about ten minutes they managed to move it and we were able to get out. But, because there were so many people in the lift I was unable to do my "James Bond". We were extremely relieved when the doors opened. We left the building by the stairs!

When we went back to the hotel to check out we asked for the bags to be brought down, and there was more trouble with the lifts! As the porter pushed the trolley out of the lift, which hadn't opened level with the floor, the wheels jammed in the gap and Stephen's computer bag did a forward roll onto the floor! Fortunately nothing was broken, but we made a noise and it served a good purpose in the end as our taxi didn't arrive and because they felt guilty, they drove us, free of charge to the airport! The taxi would have cost $25!

When we arrived at the airport, again no trolleys, we struggled through security, where Stephen was asked to move his penknife from hand luggage to a suitcase, which was good, and on to check-in. As our luggage hadn't got any lighter we ended up having to pay an excess baggage charge again. Guess where you had to go to pay, back through security! I waited with the hand luggage, they charged in dollars, but wouldn't accept dollars in payment! We were quite fortunate, there were other people who were having their dollars taken from them as you are only allowed to take limited amounts of money out of the country. They were very unimpressed.

Eventually, we were on our flight to London, which must have had a following wind because we got in before our scheduled time.

One of the best sights I'd seen for a long time, stunning scenery excepted, was Tamsin coming towards us across the Arrivals Hall. Now we were back!

What had changed in the two months we had been away? Petrol is significantly down in price, you can get hot coffee in a can and the countryside is very green.

We're back at home and settled in, spoken to all the children and family, the dog was delighted to see us and even the cat graced us with his company! And we've slept in a proper bed, with a bottom sheet that stays put and a duvet that covers both of us! We've had an all-day breakfast £5.50 (220 roubles!) I've washed up in a sink with a plug and used all the rings on the cooker, had sharp knives and a chopping board!

Thank you all for the emails we received while we were away. I hope you've enjoyed sharing our experiences with us. I wouldn't have missed the last two months for anything. Finally, thanks to the house-sitters who did a tremendous job!

So, until January, до свидания! (Da sveedanee-ya!, Bye bye!) ......

Stephen and Carol

The Pacific Ocean, on the Russian side.

YAKUTSK 2005

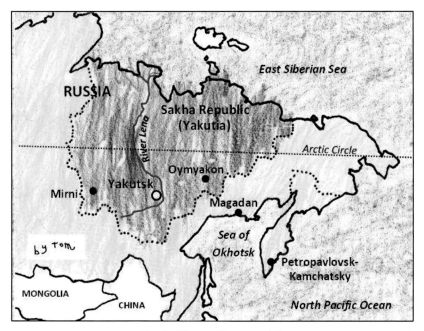

Map by Thomas Reeve, aged 4.

Carol and Stephen were not to return to Kamchatka. Instead Stephen started working in eastern Siberia, which also features in the 'Risk' game! On their 29th wedding anniversary, in September 2005, they flew from Moscow to Yakutsk, the coldest city in the world.

Yakutsk is the capital of the Sakha Republic (also known as Yakutia), Russia. The city of about 270,000 is located about 450 km south of the Arctic Circle and is a major port on the Lena River. The Sakha Republic is the 8th largest territory in the world with a population of about 1 million.

The climate is extreme subarctic. The short warm summers can be unusually hot with temperatures higher than most other locations on the same parallel, rising to above 30 °C. But during the long winters the average temperatures drop to below −40 °C. Being so far inland the climate is quite dry. The city is built on permafrost.

Sakha produces about a fifth of the world's diamonds with Yakutsk home to Alrosa, the world's largest diamond producer. Other mining companies are involved with oil, gas, coal, diamonds, gold, silver, tin and tungsten.

Yakutsk did not grow into a city until the discovery of gold and other minerals in the 1880s. These reserves were developed extensively during industrialisation under Stalin. The rapid growth of forced labour camps in Siberia was also a major factor encouraging Yakutsk's development.

Yakutsk is built entirely on the western bank of the 3 km wide River Lena. There is no bridge across the Lena which can only be crossed during the few months when the river is frozen, or in the summer by ferry when it contains no loose ice. Outside these times the only option is to fly across.

However, roads to Yakutsk terminate on the eastern side of the river. The 2,000 km Kolyma Highway, also known as the Road of Bones built by gulag labour links with Magadan on the Sea of Okhotsk. The Lena Highway links to the Trans-Siberian railway corridor in the south. At times both these 'highways' can be very difficult to traverse. Most supplies are brought in via the Lena River: ships when the river is navigable, or trucks when frozen. Hence, air transport is very important.

In 2002 Stephen was contracted to help with various technical and feasibility studies on the Nezhdaninskoye gold deposit 480 km east of Yakutsk. The deposit was extensively explored underground in Soviet times.

Nezhdaninskoye is the fourth largest gold deposit in Russia. It is remote with poor access which can take 20 hours from Yakutsk. The mine site is about 200 km from Oymyakon the world's coldest inhabited place.

The deposit is composed of large mineralised zones, representing areas of intense brecciation[11] comprised of crushed and sheared, hydrothermally altered, sedimentary rocks that have been variably enriched in quartz.

The gold ore is difficult to process (double refractory[12]) due to the encapsulation of fine gold particles within sulphide minerals and significant presence of preg-robbing carbonaceous material.

---

[11] Brecciation: rock composed of fragments of older rock fused together, and in this case containing gold mineralisation deposited from circulating hydrothermal mineral rich fluids.

[12] Processing of the ore results in a gold rich concentrate which is then subjected to cyanidation: dissolving the gold into a cyanide solution. The gold is recovered from the "pregnant" cyanide solution onto activated carbon. The presence of "preg-robbing" natural carbon can prematurely adsorb, and lose, the gold from the cyanide solution.

COINCIDENCE

Carol Lay

From:	Carol Lay
Sent:	22 August 2005 12:54
Subject:	The beginning!

Dear All

Here is the first part of My Journey with My Husband: Volume 2! I hope you begin to get a feel for this great city and country which is full of mystery, intrigue and unanswered questions!

All the best

Stephen and Carol x

Volume 2: Part 1
Moscow
Monday 22 August 2005

"Come with me a minute, Carol, I've got something to show you!"

Stephen said as he dragged me away from the business dinner we were attending at an expensive restaurant on a river, somewhere in Moscow. Don't get too excited here, but on the other side of the restaurant, Stephen accosted a man and lifted his tie asking me if I'd seen one like it before. It was a Camborne School of Mines colours tie and it was around the neck of an ex CSM guy, Scott who also happens to live in Helston. It is his sister and family who are house sitting for us... so, small world or what! This was another total coincidence - more another day!

For those of you who travelled to Kamchatka with Stephen and me in 2001, welcome back, and to new travellers I hope you enjoy our attempt to give you a flavour of life in Russia.

Our first week here has not worked out as planned but that is par for the course in the mining world. Our visit to Yakutsk had been delayed until...... we go! So on Tuesday I made my first of many visits to the Moscow office via the Metro.

The Metro is vast and all in Russian Cyrillic but very efficient. It costs

105 roubles[13] (£2.10) for a ticket which allows you 10 trips, you can go as far as you like each time, and you only have it stamped on your way in! Stephen has tried to instruct me in the rudiments of the route to get us to the office. I have it sussed - down the elevator across the bridge on the right, herd through the masses to get down the next elevators and then to the platform on the right, we need to go through Kitai Gorod (China Town), and then two more stops, off the Metro, turn left up the escalators, left again and then right out of the door... made it! Easy! The next step though is a bit harder and that is having the confidence to do it alone. Each morning there are old ladies standing at the Metro entrance selling bunches of flowers, herbs and a variety of vegetables, today there were green tomatoes on sale.

Anyway, the office. It is very civilised with four light and airy offices, kitchen and bathroom. All clean and apparently well equipped. I quickly located the coffee and kettle and began to settle in! So we began to work, Stephen handing me the accounts to do... help(!), then the photocopying, then the phone list, then... so it goes on. But all is well, nobody is watching me and I can log onto the internet for a bit of surfing, dip into my book or attempt the odd Sudoku when I fancy! Stephen's team work hard but there are other staff also in the office and I have not quite worked out their role yet!

My main task whilst away, according to our 'children' was to get Dad to 'chill'! I have managed to get him to take a lunch break each day which is unheard of and he has enjoyed but we will have to see whether it continues! He also leaves work by 6 p.m. and his colleague remarked at the weekend that they had never seen Stephen smile so much, so something must be working... Stephen says its hysteria from being in my company so much!

We have found time to get out and about. On Saturday we wandered through the Arbat, it was busy with Russians and tourists alike, and the main difference we noticed was the British Home Stores had gone since our visit last Autumn, but Accessorise was still there! Just off the Arbat, is a massive store which is like a combination of Staples and Waterstones all under one roof. So we spent quite a while wandering around there. Then we found a Georgian (as in country not period) restaurant for lunch. The khachapuri (cheese baked in pastry a bit like a flat pie) was excellent. Their cheese is quite salty and has a very distinctive texture even when melted.

There is a lot of building work going on all around the city, new

---

[13] In 2005 there were about 50 roubles to £1, or 1 rouble was worth 2 pence.

developments and renovations, and they are quite imaginative in the way they approach their projects!

On Saturday evening we went to the Circus. It wasn't the State Circus as that is travelling Europe at the moment, but a static circus which is in a very old building and was excellent fun and quite spectacular. The laser light show was incredible. It was mainly acrobatics, gymnasts and dancer with jugglers, and monkeys thrown in for good measure! There was an incredible parrot act, I never knew parrots could perform, but perform they did, amazing! Naturally there were the clowns and they were clever but I think the stars were the trampolinists and the springboard gymnasts, they even performed on pogo sticks! I would thoroughly recommend a visit if you are ever travelling through Moscow.

Then on Sunday we went by Metro to this enormous electrical/technological warehouse[14]. It is absolutely massive and you can get everything there from DVDs to orange sticks, I just mentioned them because I can't get them in Helston! We wandered around for a couple of hours and only scratched the surface. It went on and on. We bought some DVDs and then were about to go back to town when we spotted another store, this one was called "Eldorado" and it stocked all things electrical as well, I thought it was a Currys on a bigger scale or maybe Comet but Stephen thought it was better than both of these.

Then after a walk through the Sculpture Park, near our hotel, which is also near Gorky Park, we found a new restaurant. It is in a cellar, has about half a dozen different rooms and a Mexican menu… and the best gin and tonic I've had since we arrived, but don't get me on to the wine!!

The latest shop we have found to hit Moscow is the 59 rouble (£1.18) shop! We had a foray around the one under our hotel and it was a real Aladdin's Cave … nearly everything had been imported from China! We only bought some cup mats but there were lots of interesting bits and pieces - even Stephen looked around for 5 minutes!

We've had a little stroll around nearby Red Square, just so we could peek into the Moscow Bentley Garage. We wanted to see the new Flying Spur but it wasn't there. They are expecting it to arrive at the end of August, so maybe we'll see it on our return!

Those of you who remember the Kamchatka trip will remember the ongoing saga of the bed… well more of this to follow.

Bye till next week. Stephen and Carol xx

---

[14] Gorbushka marketplace.

Looking down Arbat Street.

CRAZY MILK
Carol Lay

From:	Carol Lay
Sent:	30 August 2005 09:05
Subject:	Part 2 of the saga

Dear All

Hope this finds you all well. We still have sunshine although I am beginning to think I will have to find some autumn clothes quite soon!

Have Fun

All the best

Carol and Stephen

Volume 2: Part 2
Moscow
Tuesday 30 August 2005

It's all a question of what you get used to and what you have the privilege to experience......

Still here in Moscow. The week began quietly, there are some Russian problems in the office which will probably be solved "dreckly"[15]. Anyway something is happening or about to happen in the square across the road from our hotel. There have been men with cranes working there for the last two nights, putting up stars and banners, don't know if we will still be in Moscow when whatever it is takes place, I'll let you know! September 1st is 'Knowledge Day', we believe, when the children return to school.

This extended stay has really knocked a hole in Stephen's budgeting, that and the way I keep the accounts - I can't have cappuccino and a salad or sandwich, it has to be with an omelette! However, on our visit to the Crazy Milk restaurant I managed to keep in budget and have a decent glass of wine! I don't want you to get the idea that I am obsessed with alcohol but if you tasted some of the stuff they have here, you'd be feeling the same! We bought a can of gin and tonic for 27 roubles = 54p! It was not

---

[15] A colloquialism from Cornwall; something to be done later with no rush.

even fit to brush your teeth with, in fact it began to strip the enamel! My latest G&T experience was that it came in three glasses - one with gin, one with tonic and one with ice and a spoon!

A little more about Crazy Milk. It is a bar in a cellar, quite cosy but comfortable at the same time. There are some bar chairs around the bar, and then there is a dance floor and there are little alcoves and side rooms set up with tables. This may sound seedy, it isn't, and it was originally one of the few privately run restaurants during the Communists times. We sat at the bar and Stephen said we were like two "old codgers" he with his stomach propped on the bar and me with my boobs resting there!! How flattering! We did have a good meal. It was a slightly different menu too, so I think we shall be re-visiting that one!

I must tell you about the lady doing the lawn outside the little bistro we frequent. They grow grass in the window boxes which they display on the terrace outside the bistro, and they keep it looking nice by regular trimming with scissors, brushing up the cuttings with a dustpan and brush, which is what we saw happening!

I've started learning Russian, I can recognise most of the alphabet and sound out some of it but unless it is spoken s-l-o-w-l-y I cannot understand it! Sitting in the office listening to Oleg and Baurzhan chatting, I don't have a clue! However, I did manage to translate half a paragraph correctly and translate some vocabulary so it is a beginning! Watch this space for further developments.

Outside our hotel there are numerous lanes of traffic. There are underpasses in certain places but sometimes you have to bite the bullet and cross the road. They have traffic lights and little green men etc. So when out alone I experimented. Stephen chooses not to wait for the green man, telling me we could be stuck for ages if we do, so he dodges across the road, weaving through the traffic. My experiment showed that I could wait up to 18 minutes to cross the road with the guidance of the little green man… and people wait! This morning, with Stephen we crossed in 18 seconds!

The sooner I get used to the fact that little is as it seems, the less I shall feel disappointed - for instance, as mentioned above, the wine, and now there is the chocolate… Cadbury's bar of Wispa chocolate in any other country does NOT taste the same, at least not here. There I was sitting comfortably watching a film on the MGM channel (so it was in English), glass of peach juice (remember haven't found any wine yet) by my side and bar of chocolate in my hand. I put some chocolate in my mouth and YUK! Whatever it was, it was NOT Cadbury's!

Hence my thought at the top, had we never had the opportunity to taste fine wine or eat good food, have a pick of a huge variety or fruit and vegetables, buy fresh bread daily then we would not be so astonished by some of the food and drink we have to contend with here. But fellow guests at the hotel load their plates with the breakfast selection and happily munch away. Have we been spoilt? Perhaps, but it does make life a little less tolerable in these situations. Sometimes you have to get on with it and after all it isn't life or death! Stephen says "life is too short!"

This week has been about getting bearings and sussing things out.

I don't expect we'll ever fully understand why people here live the way they do, is it by choice, habit or history? You see street vendors with half a dozen buckets of flowers, they are there early in the morning till late at night, roses mainly, long stemmed, how do they get their pitch, where do the flowers come from, who keeps the money? Then there are the little old ladies with their buckets of dahlias, montbretia, gladioli and green tomatoes, standing at the entrance to the Metro in their headscarves and thick stockings. Who is the most enterprising? I asked some 'locals' about this and apparently you get a licence to operate a kiosk but if you sell on the pavement or on the Metro steps you are illegal! Where you get the licence or how much people pay he did not know. All I know is that working in kiosks which are on the pavements, or in underpasses, where there is little or no fresh air circulating is no fun - but they work long long hours - they are open when we go to the office at 8:00 a.m. and the same people are there when we get back from our evening meal at about 9 to 9:30ish. The kiosks in these underpasses are about 2 m by 3 m! However, they are working and earning a living, I am not sure whether there is family credit or unemployment benefit here or any state benefits at all. There are big stores here too, and we have visited several, I mentioned a couple last week and will talk about others again. The big stores contrast hugely with the kiosks. There are also some stores which resemble what you would imagine to be the old grocery store in Soviet communist days, again more of these another time.

And sitting here in this office listening to Oleg and Baurzhan discussing the process for getting things done because "you must do it this way - it is the law", begs the question – "says who"? Now I am being arrogant because I am the visitor, it also makes me reflect ever so slightly on what is happening in England and wonder who has the right idea?

I am getting ever so slightly nervous now as Yakutsk actually seems to be on the horizon. Frank who works with Stephen and hails from Penzance, and Rick, who featured in my last journal, have flown in from

Yakutsk and have been saying how wonderful Moscow is in comparison! Maybe they were only talking about the weather! Frank was also saying there are quite a lot of things to see and do in Yakutsk which is hopeful, and that most of them are walkable - he doesn't like the Metro! On the other hand, Rick was saying that our apartment was awaiting our arrival and that they had gone "over the top" to make sure it was comfortably equipped for us...... The other aspect which Stephen chose to omit when 'selling' the Wonders of Yakutsk to me, was that they have snakes!

Well, that's all for this week, there has been another 'bed' incident but we'll save that for another time! Hope you are all well, 'till the next one - either from Moscow, Yakutsk or ?, keep well and safe

Love
   Carol and Stephen

Where do you think this ceiling was seen?
(Russian Cadbury's Wispa bar - part eaten - for the correct answer!)

YAKUTSK AT LAST
Carol Lay

From:	Carol Lay
Sent:	08 September 2005 07:02
Subject:	Part 3

Dear All

We are a bit late sending out Part 3, partly due to technical hitches, time differences and editing conflicts! This takes you up to Sunday 4th / Monday 5th September and begins from the weekend of 27th August.

Life in Yakutsk is different but much more comfortable up to now than you would imagine and we will inform you as we go along. Hope you are all well.

Stephen and Carol xx

Volume 2: Part 3
Moscow
Week beginning Wednesday 31 August 2005

Stephen said, "Just smile, and enjoy the adventure"

Still here in Moscow as I begin this, although for the third time tickets for Yakutsk have been purchased, and we may leave on Sunday - our 29th Wedding Anniversary! Who knows?

Did you guess the answer to last week's question about the photo of the chandeliers? It was not the Metro but inside a large supermarket on Tverskaya Street[16], rather like the food hall in Harrods! From the outside it looks like a grand grey Soviet building, but when you enter you are totally amazed! The lighting and decor are spectacular. It is upmarket and sells lots of nice food stuffs, including caviar and frozen individual scallops and escargot! We were going to buy some cherries but at £12 a kilo we settled for a tub of Pringles, much the same price as at home. We also managed to buy a bottle of wine with a label we recognised and that was quite good although twice the price we would pay at Tesco.

We went out and about at the weekend. Saturday afternoon was spent wandering around antique shops and then to Patriarch's Pond which is

---

[16] The main street heading north-west from Red Square.

where the book "The Master and Margarita" by Mikhail Bulgakov is based. This is a classic Russian novel written in the 1930's and is a story based around witchcraft but not quite as easy to read as Harry Potter. The pond has been renovated over the last year but interestingly is not as well kept as the park near the office nor the flower beds near the hotel. It was quite busy there as we sat and people watched for a while before wandering to the café named after the book and where Bulgakov is supposed to have lived.

On Sunday we went back out to the electronics market to purchase an iron now that I was doing the laundry! I mentioned Eldorado to you in our first letter, the huge store full of every electrical item you could think of. We bought; a kettle, steam iron, water filter jug, multi plug and computer speakers for the grand total of £26! Stephen said he hadn't been so excited about domestic shopping since we purchased our first new item for our first house - a dustbin! More to the point, everything we bought works - the iron even had instructions in English! Having bought a kettle we then went on to the outdoor market and bought two teaspoons, £1; two mugs, £1.60; a jar of Nescafe Alta Rico £3.38 and two cartons of milk, 40p! Well pleased with our bargains we headed back to the hotel to make coffee, do the ironing and prepare our own drinking water! The outdoor market was reminiscent of the one we got to know well in Petropavlovsk, with butchers, fish stalls, green grocers etc. you name it, and they were selling it.

This week we have become self-sufficient at lunchtimes too! Again, braving the market stalls and the kleb (bread) kiosks. A loaf of white bread cost 9 roubles and 50 kopeks, just under 20p! Then we found a producty store (продукты = shops; literally "products") which was still functioning very much as it would have done in Soviet times. It sells most food - there is a butchery counter, a fish counter, a deli counter and a fruit and vegetable counter and in the midst of it all is the cashier sitting behind her glass fronted desk. At this stage shopping is completed through much pointing of fingers and nodding or shaking of heads. The lady showed us the price on the calculator. We also visited a fruit stall in the market and the lady there was much amused by our pointing etc. but between us we managed to buy nectarines and plums.

I have been continuing with my Russian lessons, and have even completed some basic word puzzles, filling in the missing letter, but I still don't recognise much when people are talking around me - they all talk so quickly! The cleaning lady in the office practised her English on me the other day and we managed to discuss children. The problem came when she was trying to tell me about her son and we needed the help of Oleg, one of the interpretors. Oleg told me that her son was a "free range" man, which transpired to be single or a bachelor. I quite liked the term!

Bear in mind that we are on the fifth floor of the hotel! The other night I woke up and could hear men talking. They sounded very close and I didn't think there was anybody in the rooms either side of us. The voices continued and they were raised, in fact I could have sworn they were outside the window. It was noisy, I woke Stephen up to tell him because I like to share these sort of things with him! He was not impressed and said don't be stupid we're on the fifth floor! But the shouting, as it had now become, continued so I nudged Stephen again who told me to go to sleep. After I had wandered around the room and looked out of the window and got back into bed unable to see anything I fell asleep much to Stephen's relief. The next morning I could hear more noises, a cross between fireworks and thunder in the distance. So, more looking out of the window and lo and behold, there had been people outside our window during the night - they had been hanging huge banners from poles mounted just above our window and it was these banners that were like sails flapping in the wind and making the thunder fireworks noise! The moral is, Stephen should always listen to me! We understand that the banners were flying to celebrate, or mark, School Day/City Day.

We were advised that Saturday was City Day, but we saw nothing different in the city centre, there were a few stages being erected and additional tent like kiosks dotted around but no parades, no singing or dancing, in fact nothing different from the previous week. So we dropped into the Coffee Bean. I was trying to translate the menu board and concluded that they did hot chocolate. That would be nice for a change. But it wasn't quite what we expected! It was hot melted chocolate - a cup full of it. You should never guess a Russian translation!

It transpired that the celebrations on the Saturday had been very low key out of respect for the Beslan[17] memorial services. On Sunday afternoon we went back to Red Square and there was much more happening, street traders, arm wrestling competitions, strongmen bending nails, the streets were closed to traffic and the police were in heavy attendance. All very busy and festival like. Security checks were being carried out at the street ends.

However, we did leave on Sunday September 4th to go to Yakutsk so couldn't stay to watch the parade. We left our hotel at 4:30 p.m. to begin

---

[17] The Beslan school siege of 1st September 2004.

our journey to Yakutsk. Yakutsk is 9 hours ahead of Wendron time, we were booked to travel Business Class. But remember, nothing is ever as it seems! When we arrived at the check-in we were told this flight does not have Business Class, which was when Stephen told me to smile!

We send you our best wishes this week from our apartment in Yakutsk, and the adventures have begun…
   Dosvedanya, Stephen and Carol

Celebration Day. Looking towards Lubyanka, the pink building centre right which was the infamous KGB building.

DUST

Carol Lay

From: Carol Lay
Sent: 15 September 2005 03:44
Subject: Part of the saga

Dear All

Here is a bit more of the tale. Hope it finds you well and that you can still afford, and get, petrol!

Have a good weekend

Carol

Volume 2: Part 4
Yakutsk, Eastern Siberia
Week beginning Monday 5 September 2005

Sunshine = Dust!

We flew from Moscow on September 4th on Domodedovo Airlines arriving at Yakutsk airport on September 5th at 8:40 a.m. local time. Once we were airborne the flight was reasonably comfortable and went quite quickly. We had the seats Stephen had wanted and although we were told there was no Business Class we were treated as though we were travelling this way, including having access to the VIP lounge before departure. All this and we had a refund as well!

There was little significant to see out of the window as we approached Yakutsk. We flew over a very barren looking Siberia, brown, empty and uninhabited. On our arrival we were met by Yuri, Stephen's right hand man at the Yakutsk office. He helped Stephen collect our luggage about ¾ hour after arrival. During this wait, you either wait in your car, if you have been met by one, or stand outside - no matter what time of year it is or what the weather is! Thankfully, our luggage had arrived in one piece and we set off for the apartment.

Driving through the suburbs towards the town, I had my first introduction to the amount of dust that invades every inch of Yakutsk at this time of year. The countryside was what I have come to recognise as typically Soviet. I did not have such a culture shock this time, having been to Kamchatka I was prepared for the sights I saw. There are signs of improving infra-structure in some places but then the roads are still broken and deeply rutted and there are many dilapidated apartment blocks. As we approached our apartment I tried to remember to keep the smile in place, and did, but I was a bit nervous when we drove under massive pipes which presumably carried central heating in the winter and passed some very poor looking apartment blocks. We have an apartment in a new block, or is it a renovated block? It is so much better than the last experience of apartments: almost luxurious - all things are relative.

We have a security entrance, and we enter the building through a locked door. We have magnet keys to access the main doors and ordinary keys for our double locked front door. Because Yakutsk is either, dusty, muddy, icy or slushy underfoot, there is a tradition of removing your shoes on entry-which is what Yuri did when he helped bring in the luggage and showed us the apartment which consists of a kitchen, living room, bedroom, hallway, bathroom, with shower, and toilet. There is also a closed in balcony. We think we have triple glazing. We have a bed, you will all be very relieved to know that there will be no more sagas - except - that it is queen size, and the bedding is made for a 4 foot bed! We are managing however; our greatest problem at the moment is getting the square pillows positioned comfortably.

We have broadband internet which is quite fast most of the time, but I understand it can be affected by the cold weather. We also have a working gas cooker (well the hob does) but we can't fathom out how to light the oven. And we have a microwave, and now that Stephen has downloaded an English version of the instruction book, this works very well and makes an excellent cheese on toast! We have a television with a plethora of Russian programmes, but none in English so thank goodness for Radio 4 on the internet - we have listened to cricket, The Archers omnibus, Any Questions and Answers, Afternoon Play, and the Today programme is on as I write this.

The people here look at us with curiosity, especially when we are out and about and talking to each other. Most have oriental features so we look different! And Stephen wasn't lying when he said you could buy anything in Yakutsk! It just takes a long time to find it! Three days to find rubber gloves! We spoke to one of our neighbours when we all arrived home at the same time. And the security man at the office building always looks at me and says "Celtic?", (which is the name of the company Stephen is contracted to, not our nationality!) as I climb the stairs to the office.

On Saturday (10th) we went into town looking for bits and pieces to make life more comfortable, including a hairdryer and after five hours of walking and shopping we had managed to purchase most of the things on our list. We haven't really started to explore yet and already the weather is changing and the rain is starting, so out come my tights! The people here don't wear raincoats at the moment or use umbrellas; they just get on with it.

Before the rain started the roads and pavements were thick with dust, as mentioned earlier. It is a thick dust which gets everywhere and always accompanies good weather and sunshine. The cleaners in the shops and offices are continually brushing and mopping the floors, even when people are around. In the apartment the floors are covered in lino, no carpets which makes it much easier to brush up the dust which covers all surfaces even if you remove your shoes as you enter. It is almost impossible to keep your shoes clean. As the cars drive around they screech to a halt at the traffic lights on their tread free tyres sending more dust flying through the air - and under the contact lenses! The cars are completely coated in dust, hiding number plates, and you can see where they have had to clean the windscreen so they can at least see where they are going. Seatbelts are not worn here, but traffic lights and the little green man are observed.

Yakutsk is built on permafrost and all the houses are on concrete stilts to prevent subsidence, from damp or thawing ice, or any of the weather extremes they experience here. More about the history another time.

Although this is a 'new' apartment we have a few technical hitches with electrical sockets - but after Kamchatka we feel like old hands. These are hanging out of the wall and there aren't enough of them. We have bought three extension leads now, but so far none works - never mind what else would I do with my time? I will explain floor washing to you another day...... no carpet so no hoover, but Stephen would say that I wouldn't know what to do with one anyway! We have an automatic washing machine which works well, even better now we have found the instruction book! It didn't work on Tuesday morning, however, as we had no cold water. Apparently this happens regularly, and more so at this time of year, as they make sure all the pipe work is in good repair ready for the winter. The central heating will be turned on for October 1st. I think we might get a bit chilly before then!

We have started our Russian lessons, 1½ hours for 400 roubles (£8) Our tutor is called Marianne and she teaches English at Yakutsk University. It is an extremely difficult language to master - we have spent ages revising the first lesson to be ready for the next one! Marianne came with a message from her Head of Department at the university. I have been invited to teach conversational English to students at the University! I am awaiting further information and will update you next time.

As I have said, since arriving in Russia four weeks ago, nothing here is as it seems, nothing is straightforward and life here for the locals still appears far harder than we are used to in the UK, although, on the surface it seems to have improved. When you look more carefully, however, this improvement maybe superficial. Perhaps, everything will become clearer as we get to know people and the environment better. Also, because of my previous experiences I am more tolerant and accepting of the fact that this is the way things are done in Russia and who am I to argue? Therefore, it is easier to accept and tolerate than become annoyed. As our daughter Tamsin says, "If you can't change it, why waste time worrying about it?!"

So that's it for this week. We are settled, and comfortable, and having fun attempting to learn Russian and exploring our new environment together.

We hope this finds you all well and comfortable too! Paka (Cheers) Stephen and Carol

This is the approach to our apartment; you can imagine my concern as we drove up! Our block can just be seen, the browny coloured one near the rear. Below is one of the main squares where families gather for children to play.

PROFESSOR CAROL

Carol Lay

___

From: Carol Lay
Sent: 22 September 2005 06:56
Subject: Episode 5

Dear All

Attached is this week's missive. Sorry, for the delay but I have been working, as you will read! All is well here and we hope it is with you, too. Any grammatical errors are because my 'editor' has gone on strike - he says he has proper work to do. Well, I have tried to do a "proper job"! More "dreckly"!

Bye for now

Carol

___

Volume 2: Part 5
Yakutsk, Eastern Siberia
Week beginning Monday 12 September 2005

Edward Crankshaw, the commentator on Soviet affairs, wrote in the early 1940's something along the lines that it is very difficult for an ordinary Englishman to believe that the Russian can achieve such calculated deception with no difficulty. And the Russians find it very difficult to understand that the ordinary Englishman has no other general motive beyond self-preservation at minimal cost or harm to others[18].

As I begin this letter the late afternoon sun is still shining in through the living room window. However, last week the rain came for a few days and with it came the mud and the flooded roads. Lakes appeared in the middle of roads and pavements, and mud is ankle deep in places. Now I understood why there were stepping stones, and broken concrete blocks strategically placed randomly on pavements! The mud is sludge-like and clings to shoes like glue! The poor cleaners in the office block - they worked non-stop when the floors were covered in dust, but the mud...

___

[18] Crankshaw, Edward. Russia and Britain. London: Collins, undated, circa 1943, pg.104.

they spend the days brushing the dried mud off the stairs before washing and mopping them. A thankless, never ending task and at times they were making little headway.

In the apartment we follow the tradition of removing shoes so that we have a chance to keep the floors clean - as I am the cleaner here!! Our shoes got caked in mud and at the end of last week I succumbed to my walking boots as tottering through the puddles in high heels was no longer an option! Cleaning mud off our shoes and the door mat is a challenge in itself. Do we brush the dirt off onto the hall floor, to be cleaned up by me or do we carry them downstairs and clean them off outside? Such tough decisions!

A little more information about washing the floors; as you may be aware, housework is not my most favourite pastime. The apartment is small enough for this not to be too much hassle and I have settled into a routine and although I brush up the floors most days, I only wash the floor once a week. This requires me to use the correct equipment. I have a floor cloth which is specifically designed to use with the wooden pole. It has a hole in the middle which drops over the broom handle and wraps itself very neatly around the wooden 'T' shaped piece. It is efficient, but, to rinse out the cloth you have to lift it back off the broom handle, rinse and then thread it back on. No squeezy mops!

As with the housework, Stephen and I have settled into a routine, and I am pleased to say that Stephen continues to take a lunch break each day and he walks back to the apartment, giving him a little extra exercise! After work I walk to the office to meet him and then we sometimes take a walk or just return to the apartment. We are trying to make the most of the reasonable weather and light evenings but we are also addicted to watching DVDs of 24!

Last week my mobile phone wasn't working properly. I was unable to make international calls or send texts, so Yuri from the office took me off to the network provider to purchase a new SIM card. He was unable to do it for me, I had to go in person taking my passport and proof of registration with the local authorities. We queued. I believe the Russians queue even better than the British. Eventually we were attended to. I had to sign to authorise them to authorise the network provider to authorise me to make international calls! They photocopied my passport and the registration form and I signed. We were up and working - however, the authorisations only last until my registration runs out, after that I have to go through the whole process again - in person and with my passport etc. All this took 30 minutes and, according to Yuri, this was quite quick. It certainly didn't appear that my procedure was taking any longer than anybody else. I did feel it was all a bit of a palaver - but this is the way they do it!!

The Russian lessons are continuing satisfactorily - our teacher says we are making progress, but I think she is just being kind! We try to say the odd phrase to each other in Russian and recognise the occasional bit of vocabulary when we are out, but we will persevere and have homework to do later tonight! I can count to ten in Russian, and we almost know the endings to two different groups of verbs, as well as being able to recognise the gender of a word. Currently we are working on being able to put the words "here" or "there" correctly in sentences. I will try and write a little in Russian next week.

We did a bit more exploring at the weekend having managed to obtain a map. We walked down town, and strolled along a new bridge they are in the process of building. It is the first bridge to be built in the city, and people were walking right beside the work as it was taking place, stepping over trenches and wandering past the workmen. Quite close to the bridge they are building their first Catholic Church. Our mission for Saturday was to try and find a bigger supermarket, we had been lent a discount card for "Vectors" which was supposed to be the best around. However, by the middle of Saturday afternoon despite walking through loads of puddles and up and down steps and alleys we still didn't find it. I understand that because the space in apartments is limited people shop daily, but I was getting frustrated by not having any spare provisions. However, on our way out that evening we passed said supermarket and found it on Sunday. We shopped very successfully and Stephen's arms are now two inches longer than previously.

Saturday evening was spent entertaining two of Stephen's colleagues at a local restaurant, Margurita's. They were both Russian, one spoke a little English and the other none - so we had an interpreter with us. It was an interesting evening, and we learnt a little more about Yakutsk, Russia and Russians in general. One of the men, about the same age as us, was talking about purchasing and or renting property in Russia, and explained that in many families, adult children, even if married and had their own children, remained in the family home as they could not afford to rent or buy. This man, Igor, only bought his first home three years ago, which is an apartment on the outskirts of Moscow. We asked him to explain to us who might buy the expensive fur coats we had seen in the shops, priced from £1,000 to £2,500? He said about 10 % of the Yakutsk population would be able to afford the coats, but he was unclear about how they may have made their money! We asked if there was state pension for the elderly, but he didn't really answer the question but explained that workers now contribute to pension funds in preparation for their retirement.

Economics and way of life do not stack up here, hence the reference at the start of the letter. We think that this quote forms the basis of our thinking and perception of the people here. Their way of life is very confusing. Our Russian teacher, Marianne, believes that life is very hard for people living in Yakutsk. She said she sometimes dreams of moving with her family to somewhere else but she doesn't know where they would go.

It is Marianne who introduced me to the idea of teaching at the University and at the end of last week I was invited to be the part time Visiting Professor of English! I was to have a contract to teach conversational English to third and fourth year students, and would take six lectures. So on Monday I duly turned up to take my first lecture, and on Tuesday my second, and then I resigned!

They wanted so many certificates and forms, including a certificate which stated that I did not have AIDS. I spent Monday and Tuesday planning lessons and then recording the outcome, and decided that I did not want this level of commitment. The Head of Faculty had indeed "... achieve(d) such calculated deception" that I had been railroaded into a position I did not want without realising it! She said it "was pity" (she cannot speak English fluently) when I explained that I would come into the university in a voluntary capacity but she would accept my decision. So, for two days I was a Professor! But wait until I tell you about the university...... next week!

I began this letter in bright sunshine and today they have turned on the heating - we have no hot water but the heating works!

We send you all our best wishes and as I listen to the medley of music between World Service and Radio 4 at 5:35 a.m. (UK time) I sign off to sort out the washing...... have a good week!

Stephen and Carol

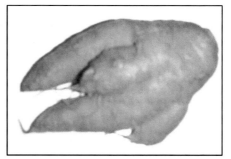

Do you know what this is?

UNIVERSITY
Carol Lay

From:	Carol Lay
Sent:	29 September 2005 07:19
Subject:	more ramblings

Dear All

Attached is our latest epistle. We are trying sending it in PDF format as we have had some difficulties with our internet and this way may be faster - who knows? Having just ventured out to BEKTOP = VECTOR supermarket I feel the need for a coffee and Jaffa cake now to revive and warm me up. The weather is definitely changing, and the temperature is down to +6 °C today. Stephen will be up and down all night to see if it has started to snow ......!

Cheers

Carol

Vol 2: Part 6
Yakutsk, Eastern Siberia
Week beginning Monday 19 September 2005

Education! Education! Education!

For those of you who emailed with answers to our photo question last week, 'a nuclear power station deformed carrot' was the wrong answer! It was a picture of Stephen's hand after he has carried all the shopping in plastic carrier bags back to the apartment! (The Tesco Bag for Life we brought with us is still going strong).

Ruth Kelly may well be introducing legislation concerning junk food in vending machines in schools, but here in the Institute of Higher Education, also known as a "university", that would be the least of their concerns!

The University is on the outskirts of the town. It is an extremely decrepit Soviet style building and like all buildings here is approached by a flight of steps. Probably in its day it was quite imposing but now it is in serious need of a makeover or, more realistically, condemning! There are about 1,400 students who attend two different faculties: language and history. I have only visited the English Department. This is housed on the seventh and eighth floors. You can reach the classrooms and staff room by lift or the main staircase. Either way you are at risk of injury due to the grave state of repair of both. As for decoration, walls are painted a pukey lime green and the doors are all painted in gloomy brown. The furniture is all wooden and very old. I couldn't get my knees under my desk. The desk had a shelf on it where there was a half eaten biscuit and some cling film. There is no provision for modern technology, there was bit of rag and a couple of scraggy chalk stubs - I used neither! I taught in two different classrooms on Tuesday. There was no electricity in either - this was a trifle inconvenient as I was supposed to be using a cassette recorder.

According to the students, their University is famous. It is good to be proud of your educational facility, and I admire their sense of pride, even if to me it seems misplaced. I was supposed to be teaching conversational English and had been given the text books to plan my lessons. Students do not have their own books. Teachers collect the text books from the stock cupboard beside the staff room, and hand them out and collect them at the start and end of every lesson, returning them to the stock cupboard. My lesson was focused on adverbials and teaching students about "identity". All credit to the students. They could speak English well, had a wide vocabulary and were able to speak in sentences. All this despite the fact that not one lecturer in the department was a native English speaker or had been to an English speaking country - no wonder they were pleased to see me!

I was saddened to some extent by the student's attitude to life and their future. When we were discussing identity and stereotypes, they were adamant that there should be a clear division between males and females. One girl, who was bright, attractive and erudite, stated categorically that she believed it was a bad thing for male and female roles to converge. She believed that it was wrong for a woman to take responsibility for the household budget as that was a man's role. Other students, male and female concurred with her. They appeared to be accepting and compliant, and I found their philosophy on life depressing. Having discussed my thoughts with other expats who know the country well, they are of the opinion that change in attitude will come, but it will take at least another twenty years. I think I was so surprised having heard youngsters in Kamchatka talking so enthusiastically about their future and how they were going to change things and get away.

On a positive note, students do not pay for their education and, in line with students everywhere, they all had mobile phones! Interestingly, the third and fourth year students followed a timetable from 11 a.m. to 7 p.m., with lectures of one and a half hour duration and a 20 minute break between sessions. First and second year students begin at 8:00 a.m.! For my next lecture, I am talking about how the Higher Education system works in England and Europe!

When we were in Moscow people kept saying how brave I was to accompany Stephen to Yakustk. They appeared to be giving one another knowing looks. Only one person, a Cornishman from Newlyn who had been working with Stephen in Yakutsk, told me I'd be okay - he said I could walk down to the river. So since we arrived here I have been trying to find something aesthetically endearing that I can share with you about this city in the middle of nowhere. It cannot be called a beautiful city by any stretch of the imagination. There is little of architectural interest, although they are renovating some of the apartment blocks with bright cladding. Horticulturally, they have planted borders and pots outside the magazines (stores) and grow some pretty petunias and nasturtiums. Grass grows and there are willow trees. (In the three weeks we have been here the willows have gone from green to brown to leafless). The grass doesn't get cut so it spoils what they are trying to do, although the grassy areas around our apartment are allocated to dogs for their toilets!

Last weekend we set off to find the river, and hopefully some interesting scenery. We found it. It is the River Lena, but it isn't a river as we know it - not a bit like the River Thames or Tamar. The River Lena is one of the largest rivers in the Russian Federation. It is 4,400 km long (2,700 miles). Its source is in the Baikal Mountains and flows northwards to Yakutsk and then north into the Laptev Sea where it forms a large delta covering some 30,000 km^2 (11,600 miles^2). It is navigable throughout most of its course and is frozen for eight months of the year. Yakutsk is one of the major ports on the Lena. In its upper and middle regions the River Lena flows through mountainous country. Most of the basin is covered by coniferous forests with perpetually frozen subsoil. The chief goods exported from the basin are timber, furs and gold; imported goods include industrial products and food.

The river we walked alongside was formed from 'small' splits which run off the main river. They have tried to make the area aesthetically pleasing to the visitor! There is a beach, and there are some viewing areas with benches and there is a new road - probably the newest road in Yakutsk, long and straight with an even surface. What do they do? Sleeping policemen are strategically placed along the road to slow traffic down! Although there was evidence of pollution on the riverbanks, people were fishing and in the summer people swim from the beach. The sand is like Hayle Towans sand but littered with shards of broken glass from discarded beer bottles. New apartment blocks are being built to overlook the beach and are selling quickly, from plan, and at high prices so that people can have a river view. They are attempting to make life more pleasant, but, by our standards, there is still a long way to go.

We came across a recently planted public garden, with covered seating. It was planted with shrubs and trees and there was a rockery. Our walk took us from the beach to the town alongside the swampy river banks and it was easy to see the vastness and nothingness in the vista of Yakutsk. We walked on into town. More about the town and shops another time.

We apologise for not giving you any examples of our newly acquired Russian skills but we are experiencing Cyrillic technical difficulties with my computer keyboard which the technician will no doubt rectify "dreckly".

We still have no snow, which is just as well as I still have no coat. The temperatures have been in the mid +20 °Cs this week, although there has been a bit of frost on the car windows in the mornings. Those who are in the know about weather conditions here are warning that if this unseasonably warm weather continues there will be problems. It would seem that if I end up on Stephen's side of the bed it will not be because I'm searching for my share of the duvet but because the permafrost is melting in the warm weather, causing subsidence beneath the concrete stilts on which all buildings in Yakutsk have their foundations!

That's it for this week; we are definitely expecting snow before long!

Have fun!
Stephen and Carol

EXCURSION

Carol Lay

From:	Carol Lay
Sent:	09 October 2005 00:39
Subject:	No 7

Dear All

You may get this, today (Friday 7th) or you may not! The internet seems to be feeling very sluggish, and a man is coming to sort it out later - not sure if that means "dreckly". Hope you all have a good weekend.

Take care

Carol

Volume 2: Part 7
Yakutsk, Eastern Siberia
Week beginning Monday 26 September 2005

In Russia they do not have roads, only directions!

Yakutsk is a stark city with little to endear it. The buildings are basic and bland, architecturally lacking in either style or interest. There is little flora and fauna, although a tit settled on the window ledge briefly one morning! But nowhere can be totally uninspiring can it? We were determined to get out of the city and explore the countryside before the winter weather set in and with the help of Yuri (from the office) we managed to set up an excursion to go to see a couple of tourist sites. After consulting the long range weather forecast we decided to book the trip for Friday (30th September) and it was arranged that we and our interpreter, Kesher, would be collected from the office at 10:00 a.m. But this is Russia! At 11:00 we asked Kesher to find out what the delay was.

It seemed that the vehicle the tour company used was not working, so they had to 'invite' another car to make the journey! Eventually at about midday the car, driver (Andre) and guide (Gabriel) arrived and so we departed. The plan was that we should visit Bolus, a frozen lake on the other side of the River Lena, have lunch and then visit the zoo on our way back! As we set off we were quickly informed that the trip was to be done in reverse and that we had to collect some fuel first...... I won't bore you with all the details but they included an hour's detour to collect fuel, two

CAROL LAY

punctures, a restaurant that was closed, a ferry that didn't sail before dark and ultimately the failure to reach Bolus! All this cost £65 for a 40 minute visit to the zoo!

It was not all gloom and doom, we had a good day out and it was interesting to see some of the countryside and also gave us a better picture of the sort of lives the people of Yakutia experience. The roads were appalling, more rut than road, hence the quote at the top! The autumnal colours of the trees and scrubland were pretty in a bleak sort of way. Where there were good stretches of road it was because "the first President, Nikolayev, lived in a village nearby", or "went to school nearby", or "his parents......".

After the first change of tyre we arrived at the zoo, which was government funded. There were about 20 to 30 cages arranged around grounds of roughly 2 hectares (5 acres) which had a river running through it. Stephen and I found it all very sad. The animals looked and sounded miserable. There was evidence that they were fed, the cages were reasonably clean but they were small and restricted. Most of the species had been brought in from the region and some were rare. There were bears that had been in a circus, they paced back and forth in their cages. In another cage there was a bear that had been 'rescued' from the wild. He spent his time chewing his paws, they were raw! Overall we came away with a feeling of despondency for the animals. It was an eye opening but slightly depressing experience.

We bumped our way further down the road to drop the tyre off to be repaired. While we were waiting two ladies walked past the vehicle, smoking and in their slippers, heading for a couple of wooden sheds just in front of where we were parked – yes, they were going to the toilet - they went in smoking and came out smoking!!

Our next stop was for lunch in a "well-known town", Pokrovsk, that had just had a new maternity hospital built. I'm not sure if this too was a directive of the first President, but I think the state of the bumpy road would have been a very effective induction process for any overdue babies! The restaurant was Armenian and it was closed. However, our guide managed to persuade them to open up for us and they directed us to a table and handed us a menu. Kesher started to interpret it for us only to be told we could have a meat assortie, a vegetable assortie or shashlik! We settled for all three to share. Meat assortie consists of cold ham, sausage and a sort of belly pork fat (a delicacy here), the vegetable one was a plate of sliced tomato and cucumber, and shashlik is chunks of fried pork with a plum sauce. It was washed down with peach juice and coffee.

The coffee tasted much like the old Camp Coffee!

And so, onwards to the ferry. Andre and Gabriel had assured us at the start of our excursion that we would not need to queue for the ferry as Gabriel's Dad was MD of the ferry company, which may well have been accurate but not of the ferry company we needed to use! They were correct about not having to queue as there were no other cars and consequently, unless we paid £300 for the whole ferry they would not sail until approximately 6 p.m. This would not only have meant a two hour wait for us, but also that we would have reached the frozen lake in the dark and we may have been stranded if the ferry company decided not to sail as there were not enough vehicles! Another example of "Welcome to Russia"! We chose to return to Yakutsk! Neither the driver nor guide were very pleased as they realised they had also lost their tip! On our return journey we had another puncture. Never mind, it was another experience and we had to laugh about it all.

From a different perspective, we saw some towns and villages where life looked to be austere and unforgiving. Most had an agricultural focus and we were informed that the government gives the people money during the winter to sustain them. Old ladies sit beside the road selling their fresh milk and sour cream. There were lots of cattle roaming the roadside and hills where they had carved out 'steps' and ridges. We saw horses too, it was almost like being on Dartmoor! A couple of times we saw people travelling by horse and trap.

Our driver came from the other side of the town, near the airport which is where we went for him to collect the fuel, and his camera. He lived in a wooden house, which our guide informed us was "partially comfortable". This was eventually translated into it had an outside toilet and although they had hot running water indoors they had no bathrooms. They either went to the banya or to their families who had bathrooms for their baths. Such a hard way of life!

There is a flurry of activity all around the city at the moment with folks getting jobs completed before the onset of the cruel cold weather. Preserves are being prepared from the produce grown at dachas. Furniture etc. is being brought back to the apartments from the dachas, garages are being prepared to house the decommissioned cars over the winter. Most cars hibernate over winter. Some people are able to afford heated garages for the cars that are capable of coping with the low temperatures, but most resort to public transport over the winter. We have that to look forward to!

But most of the current activity is on building sites where men are working all hours to complete apartment blocks, new roads and renovations before the weather prevents concrete from setting etc. At the weekend a new road was laid, almost overnight at a site across the road from Stephen's office. This new work is looking good but I can't help thinking it is a superficial surface dressing. Perhaps I shouldn't be so cynical and negative.

Well, there is no such thing as a free excursion and on Saturday I was at the office helping Stephen to move into a new room. Despite my aversion to all activities related in any way to Mr Muscle[19], I was happy to help. Had I not been helping I would have missed a spectacular sight! The office is on the fifth floor and Stephen was standing on the window ledge cleaning smears of dried on concrete off the outside of the window. I was holding onto him so he couldn't fall and was looking out of the window at the same time. Across from the office there was a building being renovated and having new windows installed. There, standing on an outside window ledge on the third floor was a workman spreading putty in preparation for the window fitting. He was not attached to anything and when he needed to apply the putty to the lower edges he sat crossed legged on the ledge, no harness, no hard hat, no regard to health and safety whatsoever! It was a shame I didn't have the camera!

We have a problem with our heating, two problems actually, apparently one major and the other minor. The radiator in the bedroom isn't working, (major) we may be able to sort this out. The rest of the radiators in the apartment aren't heating up but the pipes are (minor). This is due to the fact that the government have restricted the heating pressure at the moment-because it is only autumn, we have NO control over this! It is snowing!

Until next week we send you all our best wishes and hope you have a good week.

Stephen and Carol.

---

[19] A cleaning product.

The ferry that didn't go!

The River Lena and countryside, they go on and on.

CHINESE MARKET

Carol Lay

From:	Carol Lay
Sent:	14 October 2005 04:26
Subject:	Part 8

Dear All

Hope this finds you all well. I hear that some of you are still wearing shorts, here that would be very unwise! Yesterday was the coldest I have experienced in Yakutsk so far, −5 °C, and snow blizzards. The snow was very fine and wet, almost like heavy drizzle but snow instead of rain! The wind was blowing very strongly and the snow just got inside everywhere - pockets, under the hood, into the shopping bag. Quite an experience, but I was snug as a bug in my new coat - not cold enough for thermals yet - got to save something for the really bad weather.

It is a bit warmer today and the snow is not so heavy, I will venture out later to see what little treats there are to be found.

All the best

Cheers

Carol

Volume 2: Part 8
Yakutsk, Eastern Siberia
Week beginning Monday 3 October 2005

"People say this place is the arsehole of the world!" said Peter, a young 20 year old resident of Yakutsk.

Peter is related to Yuri who is Stephen's Office Manager and general right hand man! Peter is a bit of chauffeur and 'go-for'. He ferries me to and from the University, fetches water for the apartment and runs any other chores. Currently, Peter is studying at the University in the Languages Faculty where he is training to be an interpreter. His English is very good and he enjoys speaking it. He made the above comment when driving me from the University to go and meet Stephen at the office. It is rather sad to report that he believed what he was saying. It is his ambition to learn English, Spanish and Chinese and use them as his route out of Yakutsk. He says he is giving himself five years to get away! He doesn't know where he'll go but as Yuri is about to move to Canada he thinks that perhaps he will join him there.

Last weekend we decided to go to the Chinese market on the outskirts of the city, near the airport - I like to travel the road to the airport regularly to make sure it is still there! We picked a cold, cold day. No snow but the temperature was below freezing and out at the market it was perishing cold! I had five layers on - Stephen had not layered up so well and was very 'pinched'! When I had told Marianna we were visiting the market she frowned and wondered why. Her opinion was that it was very cheap, just the Chinese selling their stuff. She was right. It was row upon row of cheap clothing, shoes, boots and household paraphernalia! There were fur coats, hats and boots, jumpers, jackets, socks, etc. etc. Much of the market was outside. It appeared that the vendors set their stalls up daily. Their pitches consisted of metal containers with awnings. They looked cold and thoroughly fed up - not surprising it was freezing cold. Thoroughly depressing! Prices were very cheap - jumpers from 150 roubles = £3, socks for 10p to 20p a pair. There was also an indoor part to the market. We decided that if your shop was inside you were more 'upmarket'. In the units they appeared to be selling many of the same products but in the warmth and with the benefit of electricity! The market was very busy and we felt we now understood where most Yakutians purchased their clothing. There was a brisk trade in winter coats and fur lined boots. We didn't stay long and won't be returning!

Whilst on the subject of setting up stalls, I'll tell you about the newspaper stands. These are sort of awnings with a front opening and a trestle table at the front. They are erected and dismantled daily between the hours of about 8 a.m. and 6:30 p.m. The newspapers and magazines are laid out on the trestle table and pegged to the sides of the awning. Vendors sell cards as well as the papers and magazines. There is quite a broad selection of magazines for sale including some we would find on the top-shelf of our newsagents. These magazines have very explicit illustrations on the front cover and generally they are pegged up on the sides of the awning. As Stephen often says, "Nothing is ever as it seems!" So what is exactly inside these magazines we can only guess at! These newspaper stands are there in all weathers.

I was back at the University last week, lecturing on the Higher Education system in England and Europe. The students were stunned at the idea of paying fees, purchasing your own text books and paying for accommodation. At the Yakutsk University only students who don't pass the necessary exams to enter the institution have to pay. They couldn't imagine the concept of a student loan and had no idea what an overdraft or a mortgage was. It was an interesting hour and a half and I had my work cut out trying to explain some of the idiosyncrasies of our education system! Their main interest was in the opportunities that were available to young people in England as opposed to the limited options that they found available in Yakutsk. They wondered if they would be able to obtain grants or bursaries to study in England.

When it snowed last week the University was closed as there was no heating or water......! The English Department moved its base at the beginning of this term and are still settling in. They have their own staff room, and a room for administration. The classrooms are located on two floors. Adjacent to the staff room there is a classroom. I know this as there has been a huge doorway knocked through the wall. It looks as though it has been done by a sledge hammer - and left! The English Department doesn't have their own phone, which really doesn't matter as the University phones were cut off last week! I have been invited to give some training to the lecturers on teaching techniques. At the moment they deliver lectures by working through the text books, page by page.

I have started to give individual English lessons. My first student is a 13 year old girl called Liza. Her command of spoken English is little better than my Russian so the first lesson was quite a challenge for us both. But all credit to Liza, she came to the apartment on her own to meet with some stranger to learn to speak a 'strange' language! She likes R&B music, playing computer games and making jewellery. She told me about her family and their apartment which doesn't have a bathroom and that her room is part of their living room. We have another lesson booked for next week, and I have a bit of homework to do on a group called "Boyance" - I think!

Stephen is pleased with his newly cleaned office and has spent much of this week sorting out, filing and cataloguing paperwork. The planning for the mine at Nezhdaninskoye (which is derived from the word for "unexpected") has almost come to a halt. In Russia the unexpected can be expected! Due to more Russian games there is some doubt as to who owns how much of the mine. Consequently all planning and development has been put on hold.

Suffice it to say that from running a team of up to 60 people, with plans for a 4WD for Stephen's personal use and a light aircraft for company use, he currently has a team of two, (two legs and no wings!) with the others either being sacked or deployed to other projects. Although, Stephen is very stoical about this as he has been in this situation before, he is frustrated at not being able to get on with doing what he is good at and achieving his ultimate goal of seeing this potentially rich mine produce gold! However we are "hanging on in there" for the foreseeable future as Stephen is assured and confident all is not yet lost!

I have my winter coat, we settled on a VERY warm ski jacket which is long enough to cover my bottom so that I will fall on padding when I slip on the ice as I am bound to do at some time! Last week we had a bit of practise walking on ice and managed to stay upright - just! You have to shuffle or take very small quick steps in order to maintain balance - I cannot believe that some women, including those of a more mature age - even more than 50 - scuttle along on the slippery pavements in their stiletto heels! It is beginning to snow quite heavily here now so it looks as though I may get to wear the new coat.

Marianna brought us some of her preserves to try. They were interesting. She also introduced us to smetana - sour cream which we eat mixed with the jam she made from forest berries. It is much like Greek yoghurt. Whilst shopping this week I saw the choice was reindeer or horse meat. I wonder which will go best with mashed potatoes, carrots and cabbage! We'll let you know next week.

Hope you are all well. Dosvedanya! Stephen and Carol.

The view from our window. The snow has started!

THE BOAT COMES IN
Carol Lay

From:	Carol Lay
Sent:	24 October 2005 01:06
Subject:	Number 9

Dear All

Attached is Number 9. This takes us up to October 21st, so I have more or less caught up!

It is −17.4 °C here today, Stephen said it was freezing the nose hairs! Lovely thought!!

All the best

Carol

Volume 2: Part 9
Yakutsk, Eastern Siberia
Week beginning Monday 10 October 2005

When the boat comes in!

On Thursday 13th October the real snow arrived! There was a blizzard and, according to the 'locals' there was almost the annual snow fall in one day! It will not thaw now until the spring and any further snow which falls will simply compact on the already compacted snow and ice. The lowest temperature that has been registered to date is −15 °C! We have been out in −9 °, still without thermals but wrapped up in our jackets, scarves, hats and gloves. Your face stings and finger ends tingle but so far it has been reasonably comfortable.

I fell on Sunday, no harm done but I will now keep my eyes focussed on the path in front of me instead of looking around. Stephen would like me to walk 'properly' but I have a survival instinct - to stay upright! If you walk on the flat of your foot and don't step forward onto your toes or back onto your heels you slip less - or so I find anyway! When I was sliding my way to meet Stephen the other evening, muttering under my breath about "this God forsaken country" I passed a man balancing on the ice on crutches. I told myself I should be ashamed of my moaning and that I'd best get a grip! Inside the apartment the temperature is so hot that we need to open the windows.

Around the town there are some attempts to clear the snow and ice from outside the front of hotels and some shops. Slabs of compacted snow are cut away from the edges of pavements where the crossings are, but the roads are completely iced over, cars and people slide and shuffle. It is a way of life and everybody here just 'gets on with it'! We have been covering the weather in our Russian lessons and here they do not consider $-15°$ very cold, it is only very cold when it drops to less, or is it more, than $-30°$! Stephen says that he doesn't need thermals unless it is $-30°$, I think I will use mine before then!

This week we visited the Permafrost Museum which is on the outskirts of Yakutsk. It is in a part of the town I hadn't visited before, and during the drive we noticed a great deal of building work going on. There are also a vast number of old wooden houses which are habited but so dilapidated you cannot believe that anybody could live in them. We saw people collecting their water from pumps beside the road.

On the internet the museum was recommended by the tour companies but there was little narrative or explanation, merely visitors enjoyed walking in the underground tunnels where there is a constant temperature of $-5°$ all year round. The Permafrost Museum is part of an underground exploratory laboratory at the Permafrost Institute. Permafrost occurs in all the continents except Australia and covers about 25 % of the world's land. Over 60 % of Russia is underlain by permafrost. The thickness of permafrost depends on geographical location, altitude, geological structure and thermal and physical properties of the ground. The various combinations of these factors cause permafrost to vary in thickness from a few metres to hundreds of metres, here in Yakutsk it is 250 m to 350 m thick.

The permafrost tunnel we walked in was constructed in 1967. It was made by blasting and is in the ancient sand deposits of the River Lena. The walls are lined with wood from larch trees and the layer of frost on the walls is a result of the sublimation processes in permafrost, and partly from the condensation of air breathed out by workers and visitors. There was evidence of remnants of vegetation, layers of peat, fragments of tree trunks and icicles exposed on the walls and ceilings. The size of icicle depended on which end of the tunnel you were in as the further along the tunnel you ventured the lower the temperature. It was an interesting experience and their work has resulted in several scientific developments. In Yakutsk their findings have been reflected in the construction of industrial and residential buildings, roads constructed, hydro-engineering structures, and gas and oil pipelines. The description was accurate - you did only walk through the tunnel - but what a tunnel.

At the museum they had a cabinet displaying a model of the body of a 6 month old male mammoth baby, Dima. It was found in the Susuman gold field on the Kirgiliakh River in the Magadan district in 1977. For a short time the mammoth had been stored and preserved in the permafrost tunnel until it was taken to St Petersburg to be displayed in the Zoological Museum. We still have to visit the Mammoth Museum here in Yakutsk, perhaps next week?

Yakutsk is a major port on the Lena River. Most supplies arrive here via the port. When and what cannot always be predicted. It becomes obvious in the stores when supplies of food are running low. We regularly use four different 'supermarkets' depending on what we want to purchase. The shelves in all the stores were becoming sparsely stocked - few yoghurts; only Russian cheese; no frozen products, neither vegetables or meat. Hence we were faced with eating reindeer or horsemeat!

Then the boat came in! Shelves were replenished and there was more choice, including sausages and camembert. The Danone yoghurts were back and we were able to buy chicken pieces too. Suddenly clothing stores were advertising "new collections" and there was an unusual energy about the town!

We bought sausages. They were a sort of Cumberland sausage. Bangers and mash was necessary after eating reindeer - okay, and horse - disgusting! However, either I overcooked the sausages or they were not as they seemed, and Stephen and I tasted the sausages for a very long evening! It was not just food that arrived though, at last I was able to purchase medium sized rubber gloves - yippee - I bought two pairs just in case! I cannot wait to get to Tesco......

There is definitely less traffic on the roads since the weather changed. Most of the cars come from Japan, are right hand drive and they are nearly all quite new and in a reasonable state, apart from the cracked front windscreen! Many have televisions on the front dashboard which is watched whilst driving along - by the driver. However, with the severe low temperatures and frozen roads a lot of the cars get de-commissioned and stored over the winter. If they continue to be driven they are garaged in heated garages which are very expensive. It is interesting that they can leave their engines running when they are out of the car without the key in the ignition - they keep the engine running to prevent everything freezing up, but how do they do it without leaving the key in? The iced road conditions are hazardous and there are loads of "coming togethers". This, as you can imagine causes traffic jams and the Yakutians are neither the most patient nor most skilled of drivers. When crossing the road you have to keep an eye out to make sure that the cars which are supposed to stop can actually stop and hope they aren't still slithering towards you! Naturally, public transport carries on running - we still haven't experienced this delight, and are in no hurry to do so. The buses are always jam packed full and they too have a tendency to slide, besides which we are not sure of the procedure: how you pay and how you know when to get off!

There seems to be a procedure for everything. They still use kopeks here along with roubles. There are 100 kopeks to a rouble which currently is worth 2p. In some of the supermarkets they don't charge you the kopek, merely round the total down. But in the supermarket opposite the office they still include kopeks. I have just about mastered numbers sufficiently to be able to understand the total I am being asked for - unless kopeks are involved. When the cashier asks me for the kopeks I just shrug my shoulders and offer her (always a female in the supermarkets) 1 rouble. Often this works. This week it didn't, and instead of being given kopeks in my change I received a box of matches! They will come in useful as we are currently in the middle of a power cut. I wonder when they give you the candle?

In the producty there is definitely a procedure. These stores are like the old fashioned grocery stores we used to have. They are open 24 hours a day. (I lied, during the power cut the one near us closed! I'm told this is unheard of). There are counters all around the shop and everything is on shelves behind the counter or locked in display cabinets and fridges which may form part of the counter. Productys are found all over the city, there are three within about 100 metres of our apartment that we know of, and countless others that we pass on the way to the office. They appear to sell most things from bread to potatoes to washing powder, but we do not understand the system. We asked Marianna what we were supposed to do - should we go to the different parts of the shop and purchase things individually, or should we stand in one place and run around pointing to things......? She said she didn't really know either and that she never used them unless she had to! Her advice was to go to the supermarkets. Not a lot of help! But a lot of people use them and there are often queues in them as we walk home in the evenings after shopping at the supermarket.

I am off to the butchers in a minute, and a thought for you to ponder: last time I was there an elderly lady pushed past me and held out a coin to the shop assistant, saying something in Russian. The shop assistant took the coin, looked at the lady and went into the back of the shop. She returned with a little pot of something and gave it to the old lady. The coin was either 1 or 2 roubles - 2 or 4p which she had probably rescued from the snow. This is NOT a rare occurrence!

Stephen says more snow is forecast for the weekend. We hope you are all well, warm and have electricity! Take care.

Stephen and Carol.

Ice crystals on the ceiling at the colder end of the permafrost tunnel.

IT'S COLD

Carol Lay

From: Carol Lay
Sent: 31 October 2005 02:00
Subject: Number 10

Dear All

Hope you enjoy this missive. Stephen and I are really looking forward to our little break, off to Moscow tomorrow and then onto New York on Thursday. Watch out for Naomi if you watch the New York Marathon on TV - she is running for CLIC[20].

We will meet up with Naomi on the Thursday evening and then with Tamsin and Ian on Friday morning, so it is all very exciting.

It is only −15 °C here today and a little bit of snow, the forecast says plus 7 °C for Moscow and plus 15 °C for NY - yippee, no need for thermals!

Back in a couple of weeks.

All the best

Carol

Volume 2: Part 10
Yakutsk, Eastern Siberia
Combining the weeks beginning 17 and 24 October 2005

Do cockroaches hibernate?

The weather here has taken a temperature dive! We awoke to a temperature of −24 °C (outside) one morning this week; indoors we continue to be overheated although we resist the temptation to open the windows, except for a quick blast through!! Up until this week we hadn't seen any sign of cockroaches, but lo and behold the temperature drops below −15 ° (or is it above?) and they crawl out of the woodwork/panelling. Now this could be due to the fact that the people in the apartment behind us are carrying out some do-it-yourself, so the cockroaches escaped or they preferred the smell of our cooking.

[20] CLIC Sargent cancer charity.

Whichever the reason I am not impressed, but fortunately we have only seen a few so far. Any more than one is too many as far as I am concerned, but I am pretending not to complain!

Despite the low temperature it has become firmer underfoot everywhere except on the roads. It has not stopped us going out even during further snowfalls. However, we have both donned thermal long johns which prevent the chill setting in. If you wrap your scarf around your face and across your nose your cheeks keep warm as well, but you have to remember to breathe downwards otherwise your glasses steam up! All these layers however, are not very comfortable when you go into shops, you can't really strip off. Outside our apartment people have been clearing the compacted snow from the paths, they are out there at 7:00 a.m., almost before daylight. We are very grateful to them as they clear the steps as well - we are just waiting to see who is going to brush up all the cigarette ends in the stairwells, mop up the codge on the stairs and remove the bag of empty beer bottles - do you think it should be us? Wrong!

We cannot drink the tap water so we have 20 litre containers of drinking water delivered to the apartment each week. Until this week, Peter has always delivered it for us, however, due to the chilly weather conditions his car has frozen up so the water company brought it. This was not a problem – except, nobody warned me, so when the bell rang and a voice said "voda" I let them in! It put my Russian language skills to the test! I am proud to be able to say that we were able to converse well enough for me to pay for the water and give him the correct money. 100 roubles for 20 litres = £2!

This week we were invited to attend Yakutsk Rotary Club. The President of Camborne Rotary made the introductions via email and so we found ourselves at the Tygyn Darkhan Hotel. We were met by Julia who was to be our translator for the meeting. There were ten members present who all appeared well heeled and well appointed. Three young people were there too, including Julia, who has been on a Rotary student placements to Hawaii, Florida and Toronto. She gave a presentation to the members about her visits in recognition of their support. All the members seemed to be either directors or managers, one was a judge and another managed the Yakutsk Stock Exchange Registry.

Stephen met some very useful contacts which he is in the process of following up. They were extremely welcoming and seemed to enjoy the short talk Stephen gave on Cornwall and Camborne Rotary Club and were pleased to receive the Cornish flag and book about Cornwall we just happened to have with us for such an occasion! Stephen was presented with the Yakutsk Rotary flag which we will take back to Camborne. It was a very civilised meeting, far better organised than the one we attended in Petropavlovsk, but not as interesting! We shared a nice meal with them and afterwards the director of the local school for the disabled gave me her phone number and asked me to visit! Apparently, it would be good to have somebody who speaks "proper" English to talk to the students! It is a funny thing, we have now heard of three different schools for disabled children BUT we haven't seen any disabled people, not a wheelchair since we left Moscow, where incidentally we only saw three in three weeks. So where are they? And how do they ever manage to get into stores and or apartments which are all up steps and stairs? I will have to visit to be able to answer these questions. Within 24 hours of writing this we saw a young lad pushing a young girl in a wheelchair in the snow!

Back to Tygyn Darkhan. He was a famous hero of numerous Yakutsk legends who really did live around the 16th and 17th centuries. He was supposedly very wealthy and not only had several homes on the banks of the Lena but also "horses, cattle, warriors, serves, dependent horsemen, cowsheds and other servants". It would seem that he was considered a 'hero-giant'. A.P. Okladnikov wrote that he "… became the winner of the most Yakut clans and tribes due to his own energy, indisputable talent for organization and military abilities. He takes a deserving place in the pre-Russian history of Yakutia with full rights." I don't think this has lost anything in translation! He made such an impression on the place that there is a hotel named in his honour and there is also a museum - another one for us to visit!! Perhaps he was the vision behind Yakutsk developing into "a contemporary city with a rich past, dynamic present and up-and-coming future"!

I am not mocking. Yakutians obviously work hard to make the most of their city which was founded in 1632 making it one of the, if not the, oldest cities in Siberia and the Russian Far East. It is said to be older than Vladivostok, Khabarovsk and even Irkutsk. It is unclear to me, and I am still learning all the time, who actually has the vision and 'big picture' which contains 'the plan'. There does not seem to be any joined up thinking, and buildings which I believe, or have been told, are old are actually only 50 years old and are literally falling around their ears. Figures suggest that the population of Yakutsk has grown by 40 % in the last decade to around 232,000 now. Judging from the people we've met, everybody knows everybody else - a bit like Cornwall!

We have just been for a walk, down by the beach, and now pretty much all the tributaries are frozen, although the ice road across the River Lena hasn't been opened yet! It swings between $-17\,^{\circ}$ and $-20\,^{\circ}$ most days now which by Yakutian standards is still quite warm - ha ha! The sun was out while we walked and we were well wrapped up so it was quite pleasant.

There will be no missive next week as we are off to New York on Tuesday November 1st via Moscow to meet up with the 'children' and watch Naomi run the New York Marathon. It is a 10½ hour flight from Moscow to New York so we are taking some Russian homework with us and a few good books!!

We hope you all have a good week and that you celebrate bonfire night safely.

Have fun - Stephen and Carol.

The tributaries are frozen. Docks to the left, ships behind the statue.

OUT OF RUSSIA

Carol Lay

From: Carol Lay
Sent: 16 November 2005 04:13
Subject: Number 11

Dear All

Here is Number 11 - not so much a missive, more a chat about our escape to normality! However, there were a few 'sovietisms' which had to be contended with along the way - but that is what adds to life's rich tapestry!

Life back here in Yakutsk is much the same, it is snowing quite hard today but it comparatively mild at −16.9 °C, we are forecast to hit very low temperatures by the end of the week. It is actually not difficult to get out and about on foot once you have mastered the balancing-on-ice act. The worst ice is when you cross the roads and where children have made ice trails to skate on. What is also interesting is how slippery the tiles are in front of entrances to magazines - shopping malls! The steps have carpets on them to stop you slipping - it seems to absorb the snow and ice and prevents it freezing! I now understand why their shoes have such long pointy toes - they represent the front of skis!

So, mind over matter - we get out there and get on, making the most of what there is and our time here.

More again soon.

Best wishes

Carol

Please note, my editior has been unavailable so please excuse any over chatty bits and poor grammar!

Volume 2: Part 11
Yakutsk, Eastern Siberia, Moscow and New York
From Monday 31 October to 13 November 2005

Out of Russia!

November 1st dawned grey and snowy, but what did we care, we were off out of Yakutsk on the 11 o' clock plane! As planned the taxi collected us at 9:30 a.m. and escorted by Yuri we set off to the airport. At the entrance to the airport there is a big banner across the road we asked Yuri what it said and after some consideration he replied, "Get the hell outta here!".

That was our intention but at check-in we were informed that the plane was delayed in Mirny (an airport about 1 hour's flight away) due to the weather conditions - they couldn't see to land at Yakutsk because of the low cloud and the lack of technology in their aircraft and at the airport. They would give us an update at 11!...., 12!...., 1! etc. and finally we were told we would be flying at 3:30 p.m.! Now, we had important engagements in Moscow, one with a wine glass and another with a colleague and his wife who we were meeting for dinner. The delay was serious but all was not lost as Moscow is 6 hours behind Yakutsk so we should still be able to make it. Breathing a huge sigh of relief we boarded the plane and took our seats - business class this time! The champagne was just being dispensed when there was an announcement - the flight was delayed as the aircraft had to be de-iced. Now you may visualise a lot of Russians in their fur hats running around with cans of de-icer but in real life it was more organised than that, and there was a truck with a huge blow torch mounted on the back of it which circumnavigated the plane de-icing everything. Stephen says it was a heater but it certainly sounded like a blow torch when it was de-icing my bit of the plane. Whatever it was, it worked and at 5:15 p.m. we eventually took off. From then on everything was straightforward with our flight. We arrived in fairly good time and managed to make our appointment just 15 minutes behind schedule.

And, yes, the wine was truly magnificent and so was the meal and the company and the bliss of being able to wear and walk in high heels added to the excitement of the whole evening - I am reasonably easy to please. The only disappointment was that the TV in the hotel room didn't have any English channels apart from BBC24 and CNN. This bothered Stephen more than me because I was happy spending time in a bathroom where you can brush your teeth with the tap water and the water running from the taps is clear and doesn't smell!

After flying through numerous time zones we awoke very early and went off for a good English breakfast at the nearby Starlight Diner and some wonderful freshly brewed coffee and then set off for the office and another ordinary day before jet-setting off to New York.

Because we were flying from Moscow to New York we had to check-in three hours before the flight, which we did. Everything was very straight forward, including rigorous luggage searches and we found ourselves having 'done' Duty Free and were sitting in a café with a cappuccino with 2½ hours to wait. There was more searching of hand baggage at the gate and they hesitated briefly over my contact lens container and my jewellery bag but there were no problems and we boarded just 10 minutes after the time advertised. Excellent! We were so excited! This was too good to be true, and then came the announcement that due to the computers "going down" passengers had been delayed and so would the flight be! I think we took off about an hour later than scheduled. The flight was unexciting, thankfully. We watched a couple of good films and had a snooze and soon it was time to land in the good old US of A!

Our visit to The Big Apple didn't get off to a very auspicious start once we hit American soil! All I will say is it had something to do with Immigration and after an extremely harrowing couple of hours which we never want to experience again we found ourselves in a taxi and heading away from the airport towards our destination. I shall say nothing further at this juncture as it is for Stephen's book, not my letters, and leave the rest to your imagination!! Suffice it to say it was not a pleasant experience[21].

Moving swiftly on, our hotel was in down town Manhattan in the financial area and overlooked Ground Zero. It was very comfortable and because of Ground Zero we had a view across to the sea and even late at night it was still an incredible sight. Ground Zero is lit up all the time. Again, there was more wonderful wine, which went down all the better following the airport experience. I introduced Stephen to New Zealand Sauvignon Blanc which he thoroughly enjoyed and because he was still in shock, didn't notice the price! Every cloud has a silver lining they say! Naomi arrived shortly before midnight and so there was a lovely reunion and not long after this we had a text message to say that Ian and Tamsin had arrived and would meet us in the morning.

So by 8:30 a.m. on November 2nd the Lay clan were re-united and wonderful it was too - only Poppy, our dog, was missing!

The whole point of going to New York was to support Naomi and her friend Sarah in running the New York Marathon. Just as we were all there, Sarah had brought her family too and six of their friends, in total there were 18 of us! This was quite a logistics nightmare to organise and we only joined up on the Friday and Sunday. I live in hope that one day Stephen and Naomi will realise they both can't be in control at the same time and that they will learn to negotiate! However, the group of us met up outside Macy's at almost the agreed time and after Naomi negotiated with the

---

[21] Covered in a later chapter.

Open Top Bus Tour people we set off for some serious sightseeing. They knocked off $10 per person as we half-filled the bus! This was a smashing tour and lasted the best part of 3 hours. After which we all did our own thing for a few hours. We visited the Empire State Building, and having been there in daylight and at night, I think it is far more magnificent in the dark. Next we had to find the restaurant where the whole group was to meet for dinner. Some of you will know that map reading is not one of my strengths so I left it to Stephen and Ian and we found our way there successfully, having made a brief detour to Tamsin and Ian's hotel on the way. They were staying at The Girshwin Hotel which was next door to the Sex Museum! It is described as "shabby chic" and is apparently, the place to stay. I will hastily explain that Ian and Tamsin were not staying in one of the "shabby chic" rooms but the hotel also caters for "travellers" and has hostel type bunk rooms which they were staying in. Although the bunks were quite comfortable they did not recommend them as it was very noisy, but they were clean and another experience!

The meal together was interesting! We were joined by Naomi's friend who lives in New York and her boyfriend. Everything was fine if noisy until it came to settling the bill. Never mind, Naomi soon had it sorted out and the youngsters went off clubbing while we wrinklies, plus Tamsin took ourselves back to the hotel.

Saturday was spent sightseeing and doing what you do and included a visit to Broadway to see Fiddler on the Roof which was excellent! Stephen managed to sleep through it but agrees that the bits he saw were great!

Finally, the great day dawned and Naomi rang us to say she was setting off at about 6:00 a.m. We left the hotel at about 8:00 and set off using the subway, which we just about mastered by the end of the marathon, to our first cheering spot. We met a lone lady along the way who was from near Brighton and was supporting her son, so she tagged along and we ended up in Brooklyn. It was a magnificent day. It was hot and sunny, not good running conditions but great for spectators! The atmosphere was electric and the New Yorkers were so friendly and helpful, it was just splendid. We managed to see Naomi at three different places and missed her at one pre-arranged stage. And eventually at about 3 p.m. when we were heading for the "Family and Friends" reunion area we received a text message from Naomi, "I've finished a marathon!" Yes, her mobile completed the marathon too, in a special zipped pocket on the back of her running shorts! We were so proud! She was exhausted by the time we met up with her, but pleased with her time of 4 hours 49 minutes.

Everything was a bit chaotic for a while as the place was teeming with people and as Nay and Sarah had taken a bit longer than they had planned it meant that Tamsin and Ian wouldn't be able to stay for the after marathon party. We had to get them off to collect their luggage and then to the airport. As you can imagine there wasn't a taxi to be had! So plan 'B' came into operation and we had to find a subway etc. etc. These were jam packed too, but eventually and sadly we waved them off having given Ian verbal instructions on how to get back to their hotel. They made it home, so the directions must have been okay. Tamsin reported that getting to the airport had been a "mission" but that the flight had been fine. Ian said 1 litre of vodka in Duty Free was only $14 so he felt the mission was worth it!

We too had to use the subway to get to the champagne reception which was being hosted by the parents of Naomi's friend. The subway was jam-packed and so hot. We all scrambled into the trains and with shouted instructions from one end of the carriage to the other made it to our destination without further hitches. We had a lovely celebratory drink and buffet and recovered from what had been a highly emotional and energetic day, one way or another, for all of us. Certainly a day to be remembered for a very long time.

But all good things come to an end and on the Monday morning Naomi set off for work - she was staying on in New York - and Stephen and I headed out to the airport. Not before we went for a quiet look at Ground Zero. It is a spectacle, quite chilling and so amazing that there are buildings all around the area which survived. It is difficult to imagine how it could have happened, but you can still feel the devastation. The World Trade Centre station continues to operate under the site and it is eerie during the night to hear the trains rattling through the station.

And so back to Russia, the cold and the snow and the language. Our return flight to Moscow was uneventful, as were the couple of days we spent there. We flew onto Yakutsk from a small airport, and we were able to wait in the lounge which retained its Soviet decor and style. I think our flight left on time, and we were given the usual glass of Russian champagne whilst taxiing to take off. All went well and apart from some turbulence the flight was fine.

However, as we came into land we realised we were late and also that we didn't recognise the airport. We put this down to probably having approached it from a different direction. But no! There had been a couple of announcements as we were coming into land but we were flying Yakutian Airlines and they don't make announcements in English, so when Stephen asked the stewardess were we at Yakustk, she said "No, Mirny"! The weather was too poor at Yakutsk to land there. Remember our delayed outward flight. Mirny is a small airport which was developed along with the town to serve a large mine in the area. There were no signs in English, there were no announcements in English, there was little space to sit in, Stephen couldn't find any chocolate to buy and don't get me going on the toilets! They did serve us breakfast at the airport: cabbage salad, pelmeni (little meat dumplings), chocolate swiss roll, apple juice and sweet tea! We were delayed for well over 6 hours and all but lost track of the time but a 6 hour flight took us 16 hours!

So we are back! Nothing had changed, it was still snowing, the roads are still icy and now there is a dreadful smell in the bathroom. Jet lag has set in but we are fine and happy and had a wonderful time. We are incredibly fortunate to be able to share this fascinating and illuminating experience in far eastern Siberia - it is just that sometimes we have to keep reminding ourselves!

More tales of Russia, toilets and their language next time! 'Till then, we send you our best wishes.

Stephen and Carol.

Our aeroplane awaits the weather!

YAKUTSK SHUFFLE
Carol Lay

From:	Carol Lay
Sent:	28 November 2005 06:55
Subject:	Number 12

Hi All

Here is the latest from Yakutsk. We have cold, cold weather now, even Stephen is saying it is cold. Alas, the locals still say it is ok! We have one more week here before we begin our travels back to the UK after a stopover in Moscow, so lots to do - about eight suitcases to squeeze everything into......

We hope none of you is suffering too much from the cold and snow, and that all your Christmas preparations are coming along well. We haven't even heard any Christmas music yet - except I heard some on one episode of The Archers the other day!

Take care

Carol

Volume 2: Part 12
Yakutsk, Eastern Siberia
Week beginning Monday 21 November 2005

Doing the ~~Lambeth Walk~~ Yakutsk Shuffle!!

So, here we are again, up until about 3 hours ago I had little idea what I was going to tell you. I know we promised you toilet tales and Russian but that would hardly fill a whole letter. Anyway, inspiration came! It is time for us to go home - and I am so excited because I have been able to buy salad stuff. Yes the boat has come in again - hooray! Iceberg lettuce, avocado, radish, celery (very expensive at £1.80), peppers and cherry tomatoes, real mushrooms - also expensive £1.75 for 100g. There were pineapples and mangoes too, the pineapples were £7.50! This is the first time we have been able to buy lettuce or avocado. Most of the produce is from Holland, except the avocado which is from Argentina, I'm not sure where the pineapple is from. A real salad! So exciting. Stephen doesn't know yet so he is going to be thrilled too as he is expecting pasta, which he hates! Apart from the above, there were proper yoghurts too and more ham and sausages, as well as low fat milk. I also splashed out on a lime -

the checkout lady didn't know what it was! At 32p or 16 roubles it was half the price of a lemon and will just make all the difference to our G&T's! See, either I need to get out more, or go home! Think I'll opt for the latter.

It has been an interesting afternoon altogether as the first part was spent visiting a school for the disabled. It wasn't a school like Curnow - the children were frail as opposed to having learning difficulties. The accommodation was in three wooden houses around a snow covered garden where there were a couple of swings, slide and a basketball net. Children were playing football in the snow! The Principal informed us that in the summer they had a plot for growing potatoes and cucumbers. Inside, all the classrooms were small but warm and the children seemed happy and busy, enjoying their lessons. The Principal was very welcoming and spent over an hour showing myself and my interpreter, Kesher, around. The whole place cried out for re-decoration and funds to update all the facilities and books - by our standards. However, it was clear that both staff and children were proud of their school and their work and were keen to show both to us. There were only about 70 children there as day pupils, but there were another 200 plus on the register who receive two or three hours home tuition each day, delivered by a huge group of teachers. These children are too ill to attend school. They were very hospitable, part way through the tour Kesher and I shared lunch with them which is brought in daily from another school as they have no room for a proper kitchen. We had beetroot salad, sort of 'beefburger' with potatoes and carrots, pizza and some pastries stuffed with either cabbage or apple - I resisted those, all washed down with sweet, milk-less tea! Then we were taken to look at the woodwork room, sewing room and library. These facilities were outdated but they were so proud of them, I felt very humbled. We were shown some of the crafts they had produced and they were good.

I met the Principal when Stephen and I attended Yakutsk Rotary. She has taken the spirit and philosophy of Rotary into the school. They have a very modern gym and the equipment has been purchased through a Rotary project. The students at the school are attempting to join Interact, the youth section of Rotary. What the whole school needs is a huge financial boost to enable a re-build and update. We were told there was a room for a dentist and physiotherapist, but there was no money. Right now the staff and children are planning their New Year Party, which is when they celebrate Christmas, apparently they are short of money, perhaps they were suggesting I might like to donate towards it. It seems a pretty good cause to me!

There are, apparently, Special Schools in the city for children with mental illness, learning difficulties, hearing, sight and speech difficulties - separate schools for each problem. Maybe I will get to visit them at some time - but not this visit!

We have been wondering, during our stay here, why, if the Russians can launch Sputnik, be contenders in the space race and become a more prosperous country, why, oh, why can't they make a proper toilet? The history of the Russian toilet seems to be that it had its beginnings as a hole in the ground, outside, with a piece of wood surrounding it - presumably to prevent them falling in. The user had to squat over the hole. Nothing original here, however, whereas other nations have moved on and developed modern water closets it seems that here they have a completely different approach. Many of the wooden homes still have no inside toilet, but have toilets at the bottom of the garden. They seem to have little regard for the need to be able to sit 'comfortably' - this I am sure is because they are so used to squatting, often outside in freezing temperatures, and thus wanted to get the job over and done with as quickly as possible - it could also account for the elderly amongst the population having such bandy legs! Alternatively, maybe they are less reserved than us. Their need for 'modesty' not so deeply rooted. When we had to stopover at Mirny, the Ladies toilet had an open cubicle - not only no door, no seat and no paper, but it was beside a window that was walked past as people approached the entrance for the airport! It is common to have no toilet seat, here in the apartment we have a crooked one, which really doesn't fit but as with everything you get used to it! I could go on but I think you get the gist - much as we recognise Russia as a developing country, they still have some way to go with their plumbing! There is other information I could give you, but you might be reading this over your breakfast, so enough for now!

I am going to attempt to write a short phrase in Russian now, how it will email I am not sure as it will depend on your computers. Our lessons are quite good fun but there is as little logic to their grammar as there is to ours. Of course, the difference is that we know English and are accustomed to the idiosyncrasies but here everything is so new and different it takes a lot of assimilating. I am going to write about Yakutsk!

Якутск - большой городю он очень старый и интересныйю. здесь есть много люди. "Yakutsk - big city it is very old and interesting. Here there are a lot of people".

В Якутск есть большие площади и много улицы. Здесь есть известные музейные коллекции. Здесь есть три театр. Есть не поезде, и много автоьусе и машины. "In Yakutsk there are big squares and many streets. Here there are interesting museums and collections. Here there are three theatres. There are no trains but many buses and cars".

Летом здесь есть очень горячий и зима здесь есть очень холодный и много снег. "In summer it is very hot and in winter here it is very cold with much snow."

I may have got the wrong endings on the plurals - but you get the idea!

To finish this letter, I must tell you that as anticipated I have fallen over again! On the corner by the producty, apart from a bruise or two it was my confidence that was more damaged than anything else. Needless to say, Stephen was not very sympathetic, suggesting that maybe I hadn't been concentrating etc. However, it gives me great delight to report that the next day he almost had a nasty accident - in exactly the same spot just as he was teasing me about mine! Luckily for him, I was holding his arm and so prevented him from hitting the deck - could we say she who laughs last......? Perhaps this is also why the locals all wander around arm in arm! As a result of these incidents I started to watch where and how the locals walked, very carefully. In order to stay upright Stephen and I must quickly learn to do the Yakutsk shuffle! This requires you to shuffle your back foot VERY quickly up to meet your front foot when it begins to slide - simple! All we need is a bit of practise! I noticed that people were walking on a narrow verge at the side of a wide path, when I saw a couple of people slide over on the path I realised why, and now we walk on that verge too. Not rocket science, a question of watching and learning! Interestingly, there are places where the compacted ice has been cut away, this is how they remove very icy patches and so prevent people from falling too often! It is a way of life, a way of surviving.

Stephen is hoping that the temperature would drop to −40 °C before we leave so that I can experience what it feels like! To date it hasn't quite got there, but I have experienced −32 °! Cold enough! Even my mascara froze!

We have been listening to Radio Cornwall and hear you had some very severe weather at the weekend. We sign off hoping you all survived and kept warm. Take care.

Досвидания Стивен и Карол.

ALL TO BUY, BUT NO MONEY
Carol Lay

From:	Carol Lay
Sent:	19 December 2005 12:57
Subject:	12a!

Dear All

Please find attached the latest from Yakutsk and Cornwall.

Hope it finds you all well and enjoying the festivities. Have fun!

Carol

PS. Please excuse any errors as I have hurried the editing a bit and my 'editor-in-chief' is on 'Body Maintenance' today - ie dentist, optician etc. etc.

Volume 2: Part 12A
Yakutsk, Eastern Siberia, Russia and UK
Monday 19 December 2005

Ladies and Gentlemen on behalf of the Captain and Crew of BA flight 873 welcome to London Heathrow. Once again we apologise for the five hour delay and do hope this has not caused you any inconvenience! We hope you have a safe onward journey......

Yes we are home, not just in the UK but back at Bowling Green Cottage and it is wonderful. Poppydog was very pleased to see us although we think she is missing her friend Grace, the house sitter's dog. The house sitters had done a splendid job looking after Poppy and the house for us. Needless to say I have been to Tesco - nearly every day since we arrived home!

It was a long trek home as we actually got back to Heathrow, despite the five hour delay on December 7th, a week earlier than we had planned. The flight from Yakutsk to Moscow was uneventful and on time but we had soooo much luggage we ended up almost paying the equivalent of a first class seat in excess baggage - and it wasn't just all the vodka we brought back! Once back in London, Stephen had various business chores to do, we caught up with the children and some friends, which was very good, and then went "up North" to visit my family. So the turkey and tinsel started early with us and was jolly good fun too. My mother was pleased to see me and said she could sleep more soundly knowing her "little girl" was back in the country.

We travelled up to Scarborough to visit our tenants and see what the house was looking like and it was okay - we have seen it worse - and then eventually, last Wednesday we drove back to Cornwall and into rain.

So, what next? It is highly unlikely that we will return to Yakutsk at the beginning of 2006, but it is looking as though we will go to a different mine in Kazakhstan which is run by the same company. This will depend on visas etc. being obtained so we won't know for certain until the beginning of January. I am told that the climate is a "little" warmer there, but I will pack the thermals just in case.

It is difficult to sum up the Yakutsk experience. Towards the end of the stay, and during the travelling home I was reading Colin Thubron's "In Siberia" I found it a very difficult book to read. It focused on his travels along the route of the Trans-Siberian Railway, with a few detours. He had a very specific agenda to find the rare tribes/religious groups. He wrote as if he was disappointed when he didn't find what he had expected. I didn't really enjoy his writing and find it difficult to see why he is regarded so highly as a travel writer. Nor could I equate with some of his findings and philosophies. Perhaps we both set out with very different attitudes. Thubron made the people and the places sound depressing. Siberia and the Russian Far East are extremely hard places to live or exist. I went to try and understand why the Yakutians chose to live as they do. They have a pride in their country and have adjusted within it. They are acclimatised to their environment, politically, socially and empathetically. Like us, they know their country could be better. They are pretty powerless and are perhaps more accepting or less questioning than us.

Before we left, I asked Kesher at the office what was different between living in Yakutsk now and during Communist times. His answer was very straight forward: "In communist times there was money and nothing to buy. Now there is everything to buy and no money!".

Yuri, the office manager, accompanied us to Moscow. He was on his way to try and get a visa to emigrate to Canada. As the youngest in the family it is his responsibility to look after his parents in their old age and with a state pension of about £16 a month they are going to need some help! He explained that he would not be able to earn enough to support two families in Yakutsk without working 24 hours a day and then he would be too worn out too young. His only opportunity to succeed was if he left his home. We are pleased to report that he has successfully gained his visa and will be leaving for Canada at the beginning of 2006. However, he had never been to Moscow before or ordered a meal in a western type restaurant. Yuri was overwhelmed by the affluence he was exposed to in Moscow and could not understand where all the wealth had come from. We spent an interesting few days with him in that city and learnt much more about Russia and the Russians.

Well, I will finish here. I have enjoyed writing my missives sharing some of our experiences with you. Not a lot happens in Yakutsk but wherever there are people there is life, not necessarily as we know it! We had fun and more importantly Stephen and I were together to share the experiences, good and bad, hot and cold! I know that Stephen was a bit disappointed that I didn't experience −40 °, but who knows, maybe next year!

Thanks for your encouraging emails while we were away and for keeping in contact with us. We really appreciated hearing from you. All that remains is for us to wish you a Merry Christmas and a happy and healthy 2006. Enjoy yourselves.

So, until the next journey, take care of yourselves.

Best wishes, Stephen and Carol.

Rotary International friendship.

KAZAKHSTAN 2006

Map by Oliver Hahn, aged 4.

In January 2006 Carol and Stephen arrived in Semipalatinsk in eastern Kazakhstan, very close to the Russian border, some 1,000 km north of the Kazakh city of Almaty; 625 km east of the capital Astana and 560 km south of the Russian city of Novosibirsk. Semipalatinsk was commonly referred to as "Semey" and was officially renamed in 2007.

Semey is one of the most ancient cities of Kazakhstan. It is an important railway junction connecting Russia with Eastern and Southern Kazakhstan and has an airport and river port.

Whilst still in Siberia the climate is not nearly as severe as in Yakutsk, being described as having warm summers and winter mean temperatures of around −20 °C.

In 1949 the Soviet atomic bomb programme selected a site on the steppes, 150 km west of the city, as the location for its weapons testing. There were hundreds of underground, surface and atmospheric nuclear tests through to 1989. As a result Semey has suffered serious environmental and health effects from these times with high rates of radiation induced conditions.

With a population of over 300,000, Semey is a bustling university city and is said to have a more Russian character than other Kazakh cities due to its proximity to the Russian border and its recent Soviet nuclear test industry.

Stephen was providing technical support to the producing Suzdal gold mine some 55 km south-west of Semey.

The mine produces refractory gold ores; gold locked within sulphides. The gold is liberated and recovered by crushing and grinding and recovering a flotation[22] concentrate which is then subjected to bacterial oxidation[23] to liberate the gold ahead of conventional cyanide leach for gold recovery.

---

[22] The process of separating sulphide minerals from other minerals by introducing various surfactants and air, causing them to float to the surface.
[23] The process of using bacteria to breakdown sulphides thus liberating the gold for further processing.

BRAVE OR MAD
Carol Lay

From: Carol Lay
Sent: 26 January 2006 05:11
Subject: another adventure

Dear All

Here we go again! Happy New Year to all of you we haven't been in contact with in 2006.

Kazakhstan is interesting, but cold. The people seem friendly, especially here in Semipalatinsk. It is very different from Yakutsk and I don't think we'll be doing much exploring on foot over the next few days as it is far too cold. We are reliably informed by our landlady that it will be warmer by the end of next week! Anyway, it is all part of life's rich tapestry! I feel sorry for the birds here, the tits were scratching at the windows this morning, I think they were picking at the ice. The other day we saw them nibbling away in the sacks of sunflower seeds the babushkas were selling beside the road! It seems to get darker here slightly later than at home at around 5:30, with daylight breaking at roughly 8:00 a.m.

We hope that you are all keeping well and really enjoy hearing from you. We don't have broadband at the apartment but access the internet via dial up, so I hope I can send this missive to you all - it seems to be as quick as broadband in Yakutsk - anyway we'll soon find out!

Take care

All the best

Carol and Stephen

Volume 3: Part 1
Week beginning Monday 23 January 2006
Almaty and Semipalatinsk, Kazakhstan

And so to Kazakhstan!

So you thought we were either brave or mad - we are INSANE!

After much deliberation and further soul searching we made the decision to come to Kazakhstan. So, welcome to Semipalatinsk.

As with most parts of the Former Soviet Union there are no direct

flights from London, hence we broke our journey in Almaty which used to be the capital of Kazakhstan and means "city of apples". Astana is now the capital. Travelling to Almaty was in itself interesting. Before we departed we had paid almost £800 in excess baggage, which we think went someway to meeting the cost of the flight as the airbus had only 25 passengers! En route to Almaty we stopped to let passengers off and refuel at Ekaterinburg.

Refuelled, we pushed-off from the stand and travelled backwards for about 50 m and then came to a standstill. We sat there and wondered: a) we could not be cleared for take-off as it was too busy - unlikely as it was after midnight; or b) the weather at Almaty was bad so we would not be able to land; but it was c) there was a technical fault.

Apparently, the sensor which detected the speed of the plane was not responding. So eventually we returned to the stand whilst the engineers investigated the problem. The Captain promised to update us as soon as he could and also reassured us by saying he would be contacting London for advice. Fortunately the engineers solved the problem and within about an hour we were able to complete our journey safely.

At Almaty we were met and escorted to the VIP lounge as I did not have a visa, only a letter of invitation. This seems to be common practice and about half an hour later we set off for the exit trailing our six suitcases etc. etc.

Here we are six hours ahead of you. The poor driver who met us had been at the airport since 4:45 a.m. and we didn't emerge until 7 a.m. Nevertheless, he was very cheerful and helpful and although he had little English and we had limited Russian we were able to communicate sufficiently to set off for the Hotel Kazakhstan without further delays.

There was snow on the ground but it was not too cold, about −10 °C, so fairly easy to get around except for when the sun came out and melted the snow which later froze creating icy slopes! The city is bordered by mountains which are quite stunning when they are not shrouded in clouds. We didn't do much exploring as Stephen had several meetings and quite a lot of reading to do but nevertheless we managed a few short walks and were taken out to dinner twice so we did see a bit. Maybe on the way home we will have the opportunity to see a bit more. One of the restaurants we went to was also a brewery where they brewed their own beer, you could choose from several different types and Stephen chose the Golden beer which he said tasted much like the Spingo brewed at the Blue Anchor in Helston. We were also invited to share in a 1 metre sausage! This seemed to be another 'speciality' of the restaurant, but as with many Russian foods

it was full of garlic and lasted all night!! We had a good evening and our host was very generous. Our other culinary experience was in the hotel restaurant where Stephen had cheese fried in cornflakes. We anticipated breadcrumbs and thought it was a poor translation, but no, the cheese actually was coated in cornflakes!

After a couple of days we left for Semipalatinsk. You would think that by now I would be prepared for the Soviet aircraft which fly the domestic routes - wrong! We were flying with a couple of other people from the company and travelled together to the airport. Ross, who is General Manager of the mine at Semey, was saying that he thought the plane would be a Yak 40, in his words "a good old work horse". They were apparently used in the war! Now "Yak 40" meant absolutely nothing to me but the words "good", "old" and "war" rang alarm bells. He also said that he had taken this flight when there were not enough seats for everybody and he had seen people sitting on the luggage! Thank goodness I was wearing my St Christopher!

The check-in was easy, except that when one of the cases was going through the X-ray machine they called us over and asked what something was. They thought the coffee cafetiere was a missile!! The process is that you check-in your luggage, they transport it to the plane and then you load it. I suppose I should have started to wonder then how you did this.

We didn't have to wait long to board. A bus took us to the plane and as we got off I started to wonder what I was doing there. Stephen told me to follow everybody and get on to save some seats. "Where shall I get on?" I asked as the only place I could see any steps was right at the back of the plane where people appeared to be taking their luggage. Yes, that was the way on, the way off and the luggage hold. It was okay, there were enough seats to go around. It was hard not to panic, it was a small plane, narrow, I think it seated about 26. Three crew went into the cabin and we took off, and landed, precisely on time, to the minute. It was an uneventful flight thank God, but I am working on Stephen to arrange for us to travel back to Almaty by train!

So another adventure begins. I am still smiling - just! We were met at the airport and driven to our new apartment. Rick, who we first met in Petropavlovsk, and had also been in Moscow when we were there in the summer, is now working here and escorted us. This was very kind of him considering he had to move out of his apartment for us. Although the company now has 17 apartments this is the only one with a double bed.

Semey is quite a big city with a population of more than 200,000. Our apartment block is like any other Soviet type block. We are on the second

floor. With much help our luggage was carried upstairs as the lift doesn't stop on the second floor. The apartment is, in the words of our daughters, "pants". Now I don't want to upset Rick who has been living here, comfortably, for several months. But he is a 50 something bachelor, who is happy so long as he has his beer and can listen to operas (he has introduced us to the Mozart concerts that are currently on TV to celebrate Mozart's birthday) and reads Russian books. How he has lived here for so long I do not know - but he has, and he was a little taken aback when I stared at him aghast! I should explain. He never uses the kitchen except to eat a bowl of muesli, so didn't make hot drinks, has never used the stove and leaves the washing up for the cleaner. He works seven days a week. He eats out most nights or makes do with slices of cheese, salami and halva to accompany his beer. He speaks Russian so it doesn't matter that the only English channel on the cable TV is BBC24. He is a very nice guy and he makes me laugh, but...... So basically, he spends a couple of hours here in an evening, sleeps, ablutes and goes to work.

However, although the apartment leaves a great deal to be desired, we have been here three days now and I am beginning to calm down and grow into its little nuances. For instance, what else do I have to do in a morning except pick the ice off the inside of the windows? And isn't it a fact that standing in a rusty bath is good for the hard skin on your feet? And didn't somebody say that wearing five layers of clothes when you are indoors, thus cutting heating costs was good for the environment? And who needs a shower when there is a small waterfall dripping through the bathroom ceiling and running into the electric socket? I will elaborate, but do not exaggerate!

Typically, Semey is experiencing some extremely cold weather (-36 °C and below) which has affected the heating and the apartment is barely warm so we have the electric heater turned up on full and are going to purchase another one to use between the kitchen and bedroom, both of which were 13.5 °C when we measured them yesterday, so that is one problem almost solved. This weather, according to the landlady who came last night, is also affecting the gas pressure which is why I cannot get all the rings on the stove to light properly. The landlady also solved the leak in the bathroom. It would appear that the people in the apartment above had decided to install a water feature and had forgotten to turn it off. Joke! But it was coming from the apartment above and after a visit form the landlady they appear to have sorted it out. There is now a token drip and the socket has dried out so we can use the washing machine - hurrah. As for the rusty bath - well that may take a little longer to solve (we will try

and purchase a bath mat to cover it up) but I stood between the rust patches and managed to shower today. So, with a little grit and true British determination we will overcome and make the most of our adventure! Enough of the apartment - it can only get better.

Back to our arrival. As mentioned, Rick showed us the apartment and then suggested he took us for a walk around the locality so that we could become familiar with the landmarks and find our own way around. We set off and explored various little stores, cafes and pubs. We visited a pancake (blini) café and had blinis with cottage cheese, raisins and sour cream accompanied by hot chocolate, all very enjoyable. We managed to purchase some milk and water, and a couple of torches as there are no lights on the stairs of the apartment block. There is much more to see and do here than in Yakutsk and I look forward to the opportunity to explore further. However, despite Rick saying that it was only −14 ° or −15 ° it felt a great deal colder and even with the thermal long johns I was glad to return to the apartment - where it was not a great deal warmer!

Anyway, we began to help Rick move his things to his 'new' apartment which is on the floor below ours. He was happily sorting himself out when he came back into us carrying the things he has taken with him. It seemed he had done something to the lock and had succeeded in locking himself out! He was not happy. His money and passport were in the new apartment and he couldn't get in. Stephen went to have a go with the key but wasn't successful. Eventually Rick managed to get hold of his landlady who eventually admitted that this had happened before and it had happened because it was a security key which Rick had wriggled in the wrong way, consequently setting some sort of deadlock!

He was not happy and ranted and raved his way through the evening which was very amusing and certainly took my mind off the state of our new 'home'! Ironically, he had not moved his toiletries or clean clothes from our apartment so he stayed in the spare bedroom and next day the landlady had hired somebody who broke in through the window and sorted out the problem, enabling Rick to return to his own apartment.

As I mentioned earlier, we are in the throes of some extremely cold weather here. Yesterday morning I set out, well wrapped up, to get some supplies. I thought I could remember the way we had been shown and headed for the underpass to cross the road - there was steam coming up the steps. Strange, I thought as I descended the steps. It was flooded! So I walked back up to the road and tried to cross. There were no pedestrian crossings that I could see and an awful lot of traffic. I watched people dart across between cars and after a couple of feeble attempts decided I was too cold and gave up. In fact I was freezing. There is a really cold wind that blows in across the steppes and makes you feel chilled and cuts right to the bones.

So, no food. We had to go out and eat. When Stephen returned from the office he had only walked a few yards from the car but he hadn't done his jacket up and he was freezing. With so many layers on we looked like Mitchelin Men as we set off into the night.

Well, we are settling into life in Semipalatinsk. It is a very interesting city and I will tell you more about the history and the people over the coming weeks. We are probably here until the end of March and I feel sure we will learn a great deal and much will happen between now and then. So, until the next time, keep warm and we'll be in touch soon

Carol and Stephen

View across Almaty.

POWERLESS

Carol Lay

From:	Carol Lay
Sent:	02 February 2006 12:34
Subject:	a bit more

Dear All

Attached is a bit more about the way we are in Kazakhstan. Next week I will tell you a bit more about the people, we are on a very steep learning curve! Still all good fun - keep smiling - we are, even if it is through gritted teeth at times! Never again will I take electricity for granted!

Keep on keeping in touch!

Carol

PS. The 'editor' has given his approval - any mistakes are therefore his, by default, whatever that means!

Volume 3: Part 2
Semipalatinsk, Kazakhstan
Week beginning Monday 30th January 2006

Q) What did Kazakhstan have before the candle?
A) Gas and Electricity!

Last Saturday was my birthday and it started off very well. In fact we started celebrating the night before, combining my birthday with Mozart's 250th! Stephen put up the Birthday banner, Rick joined us and we watched/listened to Mozart, ate Pringles, ikra (caviar) and ice cream with cognac. On Saturday morning Stephen brought me a cup of coffee in bed then left for a morning in the office and I gradually got up etc. Then at about 11:00 a.m. while I was engrossed watching BBC24 the television went off, the lights went out and the electric heater stopped heating - no electricity! Not to worry, I thought, I'll boil some water in a saucepan to make some coffee - no gas! Um - now what? Put another jumper on!

While all this was going on, the bell for the outside security door rang and when I answered it there were two Kazakh men standing there, one with a miner's lamp draped around his neck, nattering at me and gesticulating about coming into the apartment. In my firmest teacher voice, I said "nyet, nyet", and gesticulating politely told them to go away!

Further pointing on their behalf, and gesticulating on mine, they eventually went back down the stairs and I returned to our apartment. I had only answered the door because I thought it was Stephen and knew he hadn't taken his key. In actual fact the door was not locked so the men could have come through. If they had come to the apartment door I'd have been able to see them through the spy hole and wouldn't have needed to open the door. Never mind.

Soon after this Stephen came home and we started to unwrap presents and open cards, all very exciting and enjoyable. Then we rang Rick! Rick is American and seems to be a general jack-of-all-trades in the office. He is the only expat who can speak fluent Russian so he gets called on to do all interpreting etc. It seems that power cuts are frequent occurrences, he told us not to worry and he would sort out somewhere for us to eat later so there would be no need to worry about the gas either!

By this time Stephen and I were quite hungry so decided to go out and find the blini shop we had visited on our arrival and then do some exploring. This we did very successfully and I received birthday phone calls while we were out and about.

There was still no electricity or gas and very little 'central heating' when we got back to the apartment and we were debating trying to find a hotel when there was another knock on the door. This time it was the man from the apartment below ours. He couldn't speak English but somehow Stephen understood that he wanted to see our bathroom as he had a bolshoy (big) water leak running down his wall which he seemed to think was coming through from us - remember the drip I told you about last week? Well he had a look and then he started explaining to Stephen - we rang Rick! After speaking to Rick the man left and Rick visited the downstairs apartment later in the day and then contacted our landlady. It all happens here!

No gas and no electricity = no cooking! Anyway it was my birthday so we went out to a Chinese restaurant for a meal. Rick came too! We slid our way to the restaurant which was about a 20 minute 'brisk' walk. The meal was interesting! We started with a hot and sour soup. It was good as long as you didn't try and work out what all the floating things were in the bowl! The spring onions, peppers and tomatoes were okay but it was the long slimy bits that I wasn't too keen on. It certainly hit the spot though and warmed us up. This was followed by a chicken dish and a beef dish. The beef was similar to any other you may have had at a Chinese, but the chicken was full of pieces of ginger and whole cardamoms, both of which left your tongue tingling. Their method of chopping chicken was interesting too, nothing was omitted!

The restaurant was very busy and noisy. There was a DJ and dancing, the Kazakhs certainly enjoy their partying. They love to dance, the louder the music the more frenzied the dancing, somewhere between Cossack dancing and belly dancing - very 'suggestive'. Good fun to watch!

After this we jumped into a taxi and headed for a new coffee shop to try their cappuccino and cakes. The coffee was good - the cakes looked 110 % better than they tasted. Still it was warm and comfortable in there and we enjoyed ourselves.

When we returned to the apartment there was still no electricity so we sat in candle light, five layers of clothing and enjoyed a glass of wine - Stephen even went to bed in his woolly hat! The electricity returned during the night, but not the gas which we didn't get back until today, Tuesday.

Sunday seemed slightly warmer, and we woke up to electricity and working heaters which was a good sign! We went out to do some more exploring and headed off to the market/bazaar. I had made a quick trip there during the week with an interpreter to get some meat and was fascinated by what I saw. We were not disappointed on our return. There was a mass of assorted fresh meat on sale, types separated by area. We bought a huge piece of what we think is beef - hoping the gas would return! Then we wandered through tables stocked high with pork, chicken, lamb or maybe goat and things we just can't describe - but we will return and take some photos! It was almost like being back in Petropavlovsk! There were lots of fruit, vegetables, herbs, cooked meats, cheeses, eggs, honey and sweets in a vast unheated hall. Outside there were further stalls, mainly manned by Chinese people and selling everything you could imagine, again we need to return and take some photos so that you can get a feel for the vastness and variety.

Armed with some good smoked ham and an enormous piece of cheese we returned to the apartment. All was going well until about 8 p.m. when the lights went out again! It seems that people using electric heaters were causing the system to fail so we were requested to switch them off. When Rick gave me this information you can probably imagine my response! Still we have had power since late Sunday evening, so fingers crossed

For those of you who do not have the time to use Google to find out about new places I've done a bit of research so that I can tell you a bit of the history of Семипалатинск (Semipalatinsk) or Семуй (Semey).

Semey is located in NE Kazakhstan near the border with Siberia, and is 1,000 km north of Almaty and 700 km south-east of Omsk. As the crow flies it is very close to China! The first settlement here was in 1718 when the Russians built a fort beside a ruined Buddhist monastery. The monastery consisted of seven buildings which gave the fort, and later the city the name Semipalatinsk, in Russian this means seven chambered city. A small city grew around the fort and it was the construction of the Turkistan-Siberia Railroad which added to the city's importance as it made it a major point of transit between central Asia and Siberia.

In 1949 a site on the steppes, which is located 150 km west of the city, was chosen by the Soviet atomic bomb programme to be the location for its weapon testing. The USSR operated the Semipalatinsk Test Site from 1949-1989. There were 456 nuclear tests, 340 underground and 116 atmospheric tests. As a consequence Semey people suffered badly especially where illness was concerned. Now, in 2006, Semipalatinsk is considered a busy university town with a population of nearly 300,000.

Some well known people are linked with the city. The writer, Fyodor Dostoyevsky lived here in exile. While he was here he completed five years military service as a corporal in the Seventh Line Battalion at the Semipalatinsk Garrison beginning in 1854. Abai Kumanbaulu, the father of modern Kazakh poetry, received his Russian schooling at Semey. The boxer, Vladimir Klitschko was born in Semey in 1976.

It is now Thursday and I think we are moving apartment today, but I will definitely know by the next time I write to you! This morning I re-packed all our belongings and now I am just awaiting a phone call to confirm whether the move is on or off!

Before I sign off for this week I'll just update you on the flooded subway. It is more like a heated swimming pool now! The water level is rapidly rising up the steps and it won't be long before it reaches street level. I have seen no signs of anybody pumping it out or anything like that. The steam just swirls around as it meets the cold atmosphere!

It has been an interesting, if chilly week. The temperature is much warmer now and apparently is set to remain so for about another week before it reverts to the −20s. I have ventured out alone a few times and succeeded in finding my way back to the apartment although on one occasion I completely missed the supermarket I was looking for - but that is another story. Yesterday I went into the office and met some of the staff who were all very friendly and keen to help me learn Russian.

We hope this letter finds you all well and warm, I see from BBC24 that it is +5 ° in London today.

All the best, Stephen and Carol

TENGE[24]

Carol Lay

From: Carol Lay
Sent: 09 February 2006 TIME
Subject: greetings from thawing Semipalatinsk

Dear All

Hope you have all had a good week. We are feeling much more settled here now as we get to know our way around.

The 'editor' sends his best wishes and has approved the missive as suitable for all readers. He hopes you will enjoy the waffle with the facts!

Happy Valentine's Day!

Carol and Stephen

Volume 3: Part 3
Semipalatinsk, Kazakhstan
Week beginning Monday 6 February 2006

Dear Diary

The weather is warmer and we have had electricity since we moved in. Yippee!

We are now feeling more settled in our new apartment after a very shaky start. We are resigned to the fact that the weather, provision of utilities and their vagaries are part and parcel of life here in Semipalatinsk. Being British we will take this in our stride!

Most things at the apartment are in working order now, I put up the shower rail and curtain this morning and we are expecting an automatic washing machine at the end of the week. We have a cleaner as the company do not want to be responsible for sacking somebody and I certainly do not want it on my conscience, well at least not until they have extended my visa! She did the laundry yesterday and hung it to drip in the covered in balcony. I brought it in to defrost this morning, as the windows on the balcony are iced up on the inside and there is frost dripping off the ceiling! There is a washing machine here already and whilst I am doing my

---

[24] In 2006 there were about 230 tenge to £1, or 1 tenge was worth about 0.4 pence.

best to rise to the challenges I decided that I really did not want to learn how this worked as the mangle on it looked quite lethal. We also have an address: Apartment 54, 16 Lenin Street. We can be found near the Capital Credit Bank. This is handy to know if you ever hire a taxi!

I'd like to introduce you to Rick. He gets the blame for everything even when he has nothing to do with the problem. This week he was ordering a Chinese meal for four of us, all expats. There was an English menu but it was an old menu which didn't correlate with the new Chinese one. The steam was coming from his ears but eventually he managed to order a good and interesting meal with some very unusual tasting dishes. We met up with an Australian expat, Dave who had also worked on the project in Yakutsk with Stephen and Rick. We walked to the restaurant which was in a big centre where there was also a bowling alley and billiard hall. On our way we passed Central Park where there were still a couple of ice sculptures remaining from the New Year/Christmas celebrations.

We had to eat out quite a lot last week what with one thing and another, no electricity, no cooking utensils. One evening we tried to get to a restaurant nearby frequented by other expats. When we arrived it was all in candle light - they had no power, so no hot food. As we set off to find somewhere else we passed a man who was having a wee into the street, full frontal! What a sight! Eventually we found another restaurant - guess what, no English menu, but we managed to get salad, soup and chicken and chips. There was live music too, a violinist, electric organ and vocalist, the cost of which was added to the bill of 300 tenge, about £1.40.

The local mining company lent me an interpreter this week called Altyn. She has just returned to work from college where she was training to be an interpreter. I am not sure how old she is, she has been married but isn't any longer. She is an "economist" by training, although she has never worked as one, her explanation was that "it was the course to do" when she went to college. She was extremely friendly, her English was very good and we had a good time. A Semey girl born and bred, it was her brief to show me around and assist me with some purchases for the new apartment. As we set off Altyn linked arms with me but as she was wearing high heeled boots I am not sure who was keeping who upright!

We needed a bedside lamp as the bedroom light switch is outside the bedroom. Altyn took me to a store selling light fittings and needless to say they started to sell me the most expensive lamp they had, but Altyn said I did not want one that had been made in China I wanted a Russian one! So we bought a Russian lamp for T440 including the bulb. There are T230 to £1, so a bargain - and it works. Together we explored a couple of book shops, a pet shop where they also sell plants, they had a pot with three shooting hyacinths in for T450, so I may drag Stephen along there at the weekend, and I learnt how to buy sausage/salami and salads. Altyn explained to me that the average monthly salary is T15,000 to T20,000, but Government employees may only earn T7,000 a month. These people will get government help with free apartments and electricity.

Near the park there is a long row of about six flower shops, all selling the same stock and all in competition with one another. In contrast with Moscow, where you continually see people carrying and purchasing flowers I have seen nobody here with bunches of flowers, nor anybody in the flower shops. Altyn explained that flowers are very expensive and people do not have spare cash. They cost about T3,000 for a bouquet. Here, it is unlucky to give people an even number of flowers.

Even the residents in Semey are obsessed with their poor heating and spasmodic electricity supply. Altyn explained that her family's apartment was cold and they needed three heaters to keep warm. She said that whatever the weather the Government turned the heating off on April 15th until October 1st. She went on to say that at their apartment their electricity supply had been so poor they could hardly see and that it was the same for the whole block. When they contacted the electricity company they denied responsibility as the apartments were privately owned. Eventually, all the owners clubbed together and bought a new heavy duty cable as their problems stemmed from a worn out or damaged underground cable. It cost them $1,000. At the moment the cable is suspended overhead as the ground is too frozen to excavate and lay it underground.

As we walked around the town it started to rain. In several places the snow and ice was thawing where heating pipes were damaged. According to local gossip, the Government is planning to spend a lot of money renewing the heating system for the whole city next year! I don't think I would hold my breath!!

Our new apartment is much more central and is only a 12 to 15 minute walk from the office. I visited there a couple of times last week and everybody was very friendly. They have a strange way of doing things however. They seem to get a problem and decide they cannot do anything about it, they hope it will go away. This is why Rick is having such a hard time as the expats won't let things ride. Rightly or wrongly, and I think rightly, although you may differ with me, the expats have been hired because the locals cannot solve a problem or do not have the expertise to do so. It is not a question of cultural expectations or morals, more instilling a sense of purpose and urgency within a culture where people have become used to 'somebody else' taking responsibility for decisions. It appears to be a male dominated society. The expats are mindful that they are visitors and as such have been 'invited' to consult here. There is also a feeling that they have a certain responsibility to improve working practice when they believe it will enhance production, raise standards or improve health and safety. Is this wrong? It seems to me that the expats should stick to their standards and expect that transport is hired which has seat belts, that apartments meet certain criteria with reference to fixtures and fittings and that, whilst expats should show respect and pay regard to the principles and cultural behavioural codes of the Kazakhs, they too deserve to be respected and acknowledged. After all, they have been commissioned because they have the skills, knowledge and expertise to put things right and progress the project. As with the other countries we have recently visited there appears to be little joined up thinking in planning, and a certain animosity and maybe arrogance towards those who appear to want to change things. The Kazakhs, like many other races, do not like change and have a mentality which says we will do it this way as we "belong to do"! There are a few Cornish men here and they are trying to demonstrate how to get things done.

You can purchase most things here. I am beginning to get to grips with the two local supermarkets, Dana (Дана) and Hermes (Гермес). As with Yakutsk, the security is very tight. In one, you are watched from both ends of the aisle you are shopping in, with the guards moving on as you do. Lockers are strategically positioned near the entrance/exit for you to deposit any bags so that you cannot shoplift. In Дана they have a selection of European wines but a limited selection at the delicatessen counter. Fruit and vegetables are weighed for you and then you take them to the deli counter to be weighed and priced. It is necessary to hone your observation skills so that you know what to do where! Гермес has a good deli counter, less fruit and vegetables and wine and a good selection of sweets and chocolate. Here your vegetables and fruit are weighed and paid for at the deli counter. Yesterday, I messed up and took my bag of pistachio nuts to the checkout! The deli girl had to come across so that the cashier could give her the T143 from the till, then I had to wait for the receipt from the deli girl. I will do better next time! We are trying different produce and I bought some Bombay Mix yesterday. I tipped some into a dish for us to nibble on whilst watching the "Lost" DVD, only to find it was sweet, a bit like sticky mush, but we were not sure what made the sticky. After the shock of the first mouthful it was quite nice. Up to now I haven't seen any frozen vegetables. Both supermarkets sell a wide selection of tinned vegetables which are good. I think they are French! The tinned fruit is not as good as Yakutsk. I will refrain from telling you how Stephen described the tinned mango!

Time does go quite quickly when you are enjoying yourself and another week has passed! We are hanging on in there. Work is going well for Stephen, which is the reason we are here and between us we will try and tell you something about the mine next time.

Until then, take care, Пока!
    Stephen and Carol

Ice sculptures and an example of public transport.

KAZAKHSTAN 4

GETTING THINGS DONE
Carol Lay

From: Carol Lay
Sent: 16 February 2006 05:49
Subject: more tales from Semey

Dear All

Our latest musings are attached and they come with a warning that they should not be read by anybody under 18 or over 83! There is one sentence which is a bit rude - but necessary to give you a true idea of the conditions!

Here's hoping you are all well,

Carol

Volume 3: Part 4
Semipalatinsk, Kazakhstan
Week beginning Monday 13 February 2006

♫ It was on a Sunday afternoon, the plumber came to call! ♫

I am "home alone" as I begin this week's missive. Stephen has gone out to site and will be staying there for the next couple of days, so our apologies but we will not be able to tell you about the mine until next week.

It has been a trying week here at Chez Hov El! I had always understood that hot air rises, but our apartment seems to defy this statement as by the time it reaches us on the fifth floor it is tepid, if that! Twice last week we lost heating and hot water during the day, so luckily we have our electric heater. However, this cannot be used in conjunction with a) the kettle, b) the oven, c) the iron, d) the washing machine, e) the hoover. Stephen bought some new heavy duty extension leads and I have already managed to fuse one as I forgot to turn off the heater before I switched on the kettle!

The washing machine arrived at the weekend, and on Sunday the plumber came to install it. We were very sceptical as we couldn't see how it was to be plumbed into the bathroom. The machine itself is very narrow, probably only 15 inches deep but says it takes 3.5 kg loads. The drum is tall but not very deep. The plumber appeared very confident and set to work, within about thirty minutes he was asking for an extension lead. As

122

the machine has a short cable the extension lead has to reach into the bathroom. We didn't have a heavy duty extension lead at that time but despite this the machine was plugged in to see if it worked, which it did. Stephen said or rather gesticulated, as neither the plumber nor the landlady spoke English, that he didn't think it was very safe. Shaking his head the plumber said it was "okay, okay". Stephen was adamant it wasn't and picked up the shower head and started waving it around (not turned on) at which point the plumber got the idea and threw his arms up in alarm! After some conversation between plumber and landlady and her daughter, who had arrived by this time and speaks a little English, it was agreed that the plumber should bring us a proper extension lead, with an earth, завтра = tomorrow = "dreckly"! Well, the machine was fitted but couldn't be used yet. Still, we were impressed at how well and quickly it had been installed. It is only cold fill and was connected from the pipes in the adjacent toilet and under the bath. A very neat job was (almost) completed!

Shortly after they had departed we discovered that the toilet cistern was not working, and you didn't have to be Sherlock Holmes to deduce that there had to be some connection with the fitting of the washing machine! I rang the landlady and in my best Russian explained, "toilet no work"! This time the whole of the landlady's family turned up - Rai, Kermit, daughter, son and daughter-in-law, and some other man. How many people can you fit into a lavatory? Well, after much head scratching, Kazakh discussion and a very simplified translation, the "master" would come "завтра" (zaftra, tomorrow) and fix it! The "master" is the specialist plumber. Until then it was down to using buckets! As duly stated the "master" and landlady arrived on Monday morning and after half an hour of huffing and puffing the cistern was back in working order - but it ran continually!! Was this my punishment for complaining - some sort of Kazakh torture? Anyway, Stephen fixed this when he came back from the office. Later in the day the landlady brought us the extension lead as discussed the previous day - but it wasn't earthed and consequently unsuitable! So we had to go and purchase one ourselves and now I am pleased to report that the machine is in working order. It takes forever to run a programme and I freeze in order to have the luxury of clean clothes - a very small sacrifice!

Other little niggles here at Chez Hov El, include easy chairs which are on castors and the only place you can have them is up against a wall, bedding which doesn't fit the bed, an electric stove which wobbles and has a leg which is about to collapse at any moment and decoration which leaves much to be desired. It is not a question of colour or taste in wallpaper but more the fact that the wall paper is ripped, glued, hanging off. Then there is the shortage of cooking utensils. A tin opener is not a luxury is it? But tin openers are not common here. An anecdote I was told last week about a Kazakh girl who was with an expat in his apartment: he had a can opener which she had never seen before and she proceeded to open every can in the apartment! I had noticed that most of the cans I have purchased have ring pulls on the top. On a tin of chopped ham, the key is taped onto the can so that you cannot lose it in transit. Back to the kitchen: I wanted to make omelettes, but there was no container to whisk the eggs in. Not ever having been a Girl Guide I was stumped momentarily but then remembered I had seen an empty ice cream container and voila, whisked eggs and quite good omelettes - even though we had chopped cheese in them as there is no grater! And the kettle cannot be boiled again while 'it' still feels hot! I feel certain by now you are saying to yourselves, why doesn't she get up off her "btm" and go and buy what she needs, but that is another story, which I will save until I have the stamina to tell it!

As a group of expats we seem to gather on a Friday evening and have a good moan about pretty much everything that is happening here. The group consists of English, Cornish, Australian, American and South African men. There are some positives and one of the guys felt he had "inched" forwards last week but had been struggling trying to teach his workforce about teamwork and project ownership. He said he had floundered when he tried to explain ownership as few of his men owned anything! I mainly listen as much of the chat is obviously about their work but I hear the same sort of disgruntled mutterings each week so think it is time somebody from the outside started to rattle a few cages I   wonder who could take that on?

There seems to be some commonality with the problems here and problems we have encountered in other parts of the Former Soviet Union. Language must have something to do with it as some meanings may be lost or confused in translation but at the root there is a distinct difference in working principles and ethics. "Teamwork", a word which is common jargon in Britain, and something which most businesses and companies aspire to do and do well, is not part of the psyche in the Former Soviet Union. It is hard work to impart both philosophically and in practice to encourage participation. Teamwork requires a certain amount of mutual trust and respect, but in addition each team player needs to demonstrate an interest and willingness to do their job well; to the benefit of others, enabling them to also successfully achieve their target.

Communication difficulties are only a small part of the problem.

Transport and translators seems to worry the guys as well. There do not seem to be enough cars, drivers and interpreters with technical skills to go around. People are making do, which is adding to their frustrations at not being able to get where they need to be to gather the information they want in order to complete their jobs properly and go home! You can add accommodation discomforts to the list of moans as well. The local mine operating company now rents 19 apartments. They have rented the one we are in for two years. Last week we met somebody who had lived here and he ran through the list of complaints he had then - and guess what, they are on our list too. However, few of the men are accompanied by their wives or partners so they just put up with the lack of facilities and reserve their energies for coping with their work and drinking beer so that they don't notice their surroundings too much! But I have the time to complain and indeed, I see it as my duty to try and change things. How can the company carry on ignoring the men's complaints - they are all justified and nobody is asking for luxuries, just that their apartments are comfortable and functional. One of the South African guys commented that when he arrived here he was "unpleasantly surprised" at the conditions he was expected to live in. It makes sense to me, that if the expats can return to their apartments and relax then they will be rested and ready for another day at the rock face. Safety standards are not of apparent importance, cars are hired without seatbelts and when asked drivers respond with, "Don't worry, I am a very good driver"!! When I was in the office at the weekend I saw a light switch taped to the wall! In the toilet there was a sign, in Russian, on the wall. I can guess what it says, and Stephen says he prefers to remain in ignorance, but what would it take to add a translation? It sounds arrogant, but if people know no different how can they know what they might want to change or aspire to?

We had some very 'mild' weather towards the end of last week, which was pleasant to be out in but made walking treacherous. Thawed snow became slushy deep puddles and it is crucial to remember only to walk where you can see footprints already, otherwise you are in wet water up to your ankles - I speak from experience! I told Stephen that I was impressed because people had been spreading grit on the pavements outside their shops. Stephen smiled and explained that that was the pavement! The walk to and from the office was quite an expedition and challenge and Jack, an American expat, said it was "slicker than a licked nipple"! It limited our explorations but on Sunday the temperature dived again making it much firmer under foot and so we went for a wander through Victory Park and much to Stephen's delight I introduced him to the inside of the Dana supermarket!

There is a sense of community amongst the expats but I have not been here long enough to know whether this is extended to functions where the whole workforce is together socially. Certainly, nobody has mentioned any, but time will tell. Most of the guys eat out each evening. We eat out two or three times a week and for a basic two course meal with wine and beer we pay less than T1,500 = £6.50 altogether. They make good salads here but loads of garlic is prevalent in most meals. Few of the locals eat out as they consider it too expensive, and you rarely see couples other than 'courting couples'. Tables usually consist of groups of men or groups of women. Even the women drink beer and many smoke.

I think my visa has been extended. My passport had to be taken for a three hour drive to Ust'-Kamenogorsk, and back, to have this processed. It was valid until the 18th February and I was informed I would get it back on the 22nd. "Has it definitely been extended?" I asked. "They said it would be" was the response. Not impressed, I asked for it to be collected and returned to me pronto! Today I have received an email informing me that my passport is back in the office and now all that remains is that it is taken to the authorities to re-register me here as resident in Semipalatinsk! So much red tape. But it looks as though I am not going to be an illegal immigrant, phew!

Well, I am longing for a coffee now and the washing machine programme is almost finished, so coffee and then heater and then it will be time to prepare for a Russian lesson. The sun is shining in through the windows and the ice is thawing from the window panes, birds are chipping away at the melting ice on the window ledge - all is well in the world and especially Semipalatinsk!

Signing off for now, have a good week,
Stephen and Carol.

GOLDEN SMILE

Carol Lay

From:	Carol Lay
Sent:	28 February 2006 12:14
Subject:	some more tales

Dear All

Please find attached the next bit of the saga and we hope it finds you all well. We, (the royal "we") apologise for the lack of mining information, my 'editor' is obviously reserving it for his book!

It is −10 °C here today and I am reliably informed that tomorrow is the first day of Spring in Semipalatinsk. They will be eating pancakes all week which they fill with jam or caviar or sour cream (сметана/smetana). In Semipalatinsk each of the four seasons lasts exactly three months, hence, Spring begins on March 1st.

We have been plagued with power cuts at the apartment so I am sitting beside the electric heater with my thermals under my clothes, looking forward to getting back to England - it has to be warmer than here!

We send you all our best wishes and please, keep in touch!

Love

Carol and Stephen

Volume 3: Part 5
Semipalatinsk, Kazakhstan
Week beginning Monday 20 February 2006

Shall I let you into a secret......?

My new Russian tutor is really impressed with my progress, she tells me I read well and that I am memorising the vocabulary very quickly! The secret is, I haven't told her I have had lessons before - oh yes I too can be as devious as those around me!!

Due to the lack of ingredients to make a substantial meal we have been eating out quite a lot recently at our local restaurant, called the 'час пик', (chas pik, or "Rush Hour"). They are so used to the expats that they have re-written the menu in English and as soon as they walk in fetch them a beer! It is one of the few places where you can buy wine by the glass. It is not very good wine but needs must, and all that! The last time we went there and asked for the wine we were told "нет" (nyet, no), and they explained via the menu they only had white wine, so I tried it, it was like sherry, and okay, but the waitress thought it was very funny so I am not altogether sure what I was drinking!

Wherever you live on this planet, the idea of getting out of life what you put into it is as true here as anywhere else. We arrived here in January more by default than by intent after the breakdown in negotiations at the Nezhdaninskoye Mine in Yakutia which culminated in the company selling their share in the mine earlier this year. The operating mine here, Suzdal is in production and the General Manager who came here last summer was having difficulty coping with the huge workload. Stephen was asked to come here and assist, applying his breadth of experience at working in Russia and the Former Soviet Union. Determined to do a good job and crack on we put much effort into settling in and making the most of the poor and limited facilities we were subjected too, both domestically, and for Stephen, in the workplace.

We understand that there are certain things over which no individual, other than a Government minister, has any power or influence, such as determining who shall or shall not have hot water, heating, electricity, gas, safe roads, ice free pavements. And as such we overcome these minor irritations and make the best of what there actually is. But there are other things which could be changed to make life better IF there is a will to do so. "IF": a little word with such a big meaning. In Russian it is "если!"(yesli, if). I am disappointed to say that we are hitting the "can't do" attitude constantly and have yet to encounter the "how can we" optimism. This has had a very harsh impact on us and other expats recently, possibly to an extent when work is being seriously affected and consultant's integrity questioned. I am not just talking about Stephen's work, but work that is being undertaken both here in the city office and out at the site, mainly by the expats who have been hired for their knowledge as neither the skill nor know-how is here amongst the in-country workers.

Naturally, I am biased and will always fight Stephen's corner for him, but to see other expats demoralised by their treatment is hard to sit and watch silently! There is a highly skilled in-country workforce, who understand the structures and strategies which underpin their way of working; the need for written authority to make decisions; the expectation that you will write to seek permission to complete your work; the acceptance that only certain people can detour a 'system'; the idea that there is no expectation for an individual to make a decision, simply to do what they have been asked to do. This is all well and fine, and I am not arguing it, but I would be brave enough to suggest IF they (the Kazakhs) did have sufficient, knowledge, skill and money they would never have entertained the thought of an English company owning their mine in the first place! Pride in your company should be commended but the workforce needs to also be enabled to understand that they have others in whom they should be proud too, as without their input they would not have bread to put on the table even if it is only T25 a loaf.

We have met this attitude at other mines, and Stephen has learnt how to work with it, however at no time has he tried to infiltrate and become "one of them". He is wise enough to acknowledge that this could never ever happen. It is not like eventually being accepted as Cornish after living in the county for about 30 years!! It is naive to even contemplate that you could ever be "one of them". Indeed "they" are much more artful and will play the person who attempts to infiltrate their ranks extremely skilfully, and probably without the player realising until it is too late. Respecting one another's culture and heritage is paramount where there is any joint working but why would you want to lose your own sense of identity?

How could I ever have thought Yakutsk was a poor city? In comparison with Semipalatinsk it is like Monte Carlo! Okay, the weather was an absolute challenge, with literally experiencing being chilled to the bone and there was no fresh meat or decent wine but they were trying to improve their infrastructure, and trying to replace crumbling and shoddy buildings. Here they may have fresh meat and passable wine but their infrastructure and buildings programme is not very well developed, in fact the city seems severely developmentally delayed.

We slithered back to the market last weekend, a bit like Derby and Joan, holding each other up! We weren't disappointed and returned well stocked up with pork, lamb, chicken and other fresh produce. We are pretty sure you are supposed to haggle over prices but with our limited linguistic skills we just paid up and got the hell out of there! Since then I have learnt the correct way to ask how much a product is: сколько ето стоит? (skolka eta stoit). With so much meat to sell I do not understand why there is no butcher in the centre of the town.

Apart from our market visit we also attempted to shop for an additional heater on Sunday. It had to be a fan heater so that it could be used when the washing machine, or oven, etc. were in use but we were amazed to find that most of the stores closed on a Sunday so after traipsing the length and breadth of the slippery city we gave up and I managed to get one from the store across the road from the apartment on Monday morning! Now we are much more comfortable. Such a luxury!

We dropped into the coffee shop near the apartment at the weekend in search of a cappuccino and not only did we have a big one (большой/bolshoy, as in the ballet), but also an English breakfast! This consisted of some chopped smoked streaky bacon, an omelette, toast and barbeque sauce. The breakfast was £1 and the cappuccino £1.50. It made a change and was quite good. We did wonder who had taught or told the waitress/chef what a cappo should look or taste like and ditto with the breakfast, and at the same time with only a handful of English people in the town why should they want to sell such a breakfast?

I am not sure if I told you that I got locked into the apartment a couple of times last week and after the unhelpful suggestion of putting some grease on the lock so that it didn't happen again (this said while I was still locked in). I insisted on having the locks changed. Such a demanding person am I, that I demanded it was done that afternoon. We are on the fifth floor of an apartment block, my Russian tutor said, "Кэрол, (Carol) you are in much danger!" Thankfully, the landlady concurred with this statement and within a couple of hours we had new locks, which so far have worked very effectively. I have also learnt that when somebody rings the doorbell I must say "кто ето?" (who is it?) Instead of shouting - "speak English or go away!"

Another contrast between Semipalatinsk and Yakutsk is that although there was more wealth in Yakutsk, with Yakutia being an area rich in minerals and the consequent prosperity, the people did not appear to be outwardly happy. Here you see people laughing and joking in shops, the streets, cafes and definitely at the market! Everywhere you looked at the market you glimpsed wonderful golden grins. The dentists here must do a roaring trade in gold fillings and caps! People's mouths glint in the sunlight!

There was a growing development of western type shopping malls in Yakutsk with 'designer' stores popping up all over the town. Whilst here the shops are still very Soviet in design and content, with most people shopping for their clothing and homewares at the market. My Russian tutor informed me that most normal people, like her, do not shop at the supermarkets as they are for rich people! They shop at the market and the little grocery shops which are near all the apartment blocks or at the producty which as I have mentioned before, is like the old village grocers with a bit of everything. In addition to groceries most of the producty in Semey also sell mobile phones.

An interesting point we have found out is that when somebody is unwell and needs to be off work they go to the hospital for the daytime and are allowed home in the evening! I was getting a bit confused as to why so many of the workforce were spending time in hospital and when I asked if they were better they just showed me a patch of eczema or rubbed their tummy. Even for a cold you stay off work and in the hospital! Imagine the state of the NHS if we did this!

I have only one more week in Kazakhstan as I am returning to the UK at the beginning of March. Stephen will follow me a couple of weeks or so later. Due to administrative wrangling and interference we have not been able to get out of the city at all, so I have been unable to get a glimpse of country life in Kazakhstan. This is a shame but is just one of those things.

So, I/we will not be sorry to leave Semipalatinsk, with all its quirks and foibles. We have met some good and interesting people but the state of the infrastructure and living conditions we have been subjected to have been harsh and hazardous. Missing manhole covers, which are mainly identified by the steam rising from them, making them difficult to see in the dark; subway steps covered in ice which is never removed and people continually slip and slide on them - no wonder the hospitals are so full; unlit stairwells in apartment blocks; sockets which flash blue as you swap your electrical appliances. If this is the way of life you are used to and are unable to challenge or change, or are too tired trying to, then you have no choice but to put up with it.

But we have a choice and a return ticket to home. This has certainly been a character building experience for which I am truly grateful! I will never, ever, ever take anything normal like: electricity and hot and cold water, and supermarkets, and proper double beds with double bed sized bedding, and clothes that don't smell of grease, grime and garlic, and driving to the shops and doing all my shopping in one place without putting my bags in a locker, for granted again - well at least not for a week or two!

I apologise for the lack of excitement on this journey, but believe me if I had told you the whole story your hair would be standing on end! I will be back, I am not sure whether you view this as a threat or a promise, but it will be a surprise - for all of us!!

MOVING ON

Carol Lay

From: Carol Lay
Sent: 29 March 2006 16:45
Subject: Do you want to know a secret?

Dear All

Attached is our latest news, as you will read we were sworn to secrecy as there were several deals happening which hinged to some extent on Stephen's presence, integrity and name.

However, as it is now public we wanted to share it with you as you have all been such good friends and supports over the last few months - some of which were a bit tricky at times!

Nevertheless, we both feel far stronger characters for the experience......
sort of, honest! I am far more patient, fortunately for Stephen, although he says I am still a nutter - not quite sure what he means......!

I am very excited for Stephen and also for myself as all sorts of opportunities are beginning to emerge - so all I can say is watch this space!

Thank you so much for keeping in touch, it meant such a lot to us both and we look forward to seeing you all in person in the near future.

Till then, take care

Stephen and Carol

Volume 3: The Epilogue
UK
Wednesday March 29th 2006

You may have wondered why......?

Well, so we are back in the jolly old United Kingdom, and it is great despite the rain and the wind and the fact that we are still living in hotels!

Stephen and I have left the trials and tribulations of the frozen Former Soviet Union and waved a gleeful goodbye to the ice, snow and shish kebabs and we are tentatively tiptoeing towards warmer climes!

And you may have been wondering why on earth we were putting up with it. Christmas was a time for reflecting especially as Stephen was being offered some sensible jobs in sensible places. An "appeal to your sense of loyalty" was made to get us to go to Kazakhstan "where you will be well looked after". Well you know that part of the story!

During our time in Kazakhstan Stephen was working out his notice. He had been asked not to make any announcements and nobody except the MD of the London company knew until the day before he left!

On 17th March Stephen left the company after 4 years and on 20th March he began working for another London listed company as their Chief Executive Officer working out of offices in London. The official announcement has already been published in various mining pages. This company has rights to major coal deposits reputed to be "one of the world's largest energy banks" just outside Adelaide. So, at last a warm climate (I think it will be one extreme to the other) and people who sort of speak English!

We are now patiently waiting to be 'sent' to Sydney and then onto Adelaide and Perth, hence we remain in London to be ready to fly off at a moment's notice - the flight socks and aspirin are ready and waiting as are the empty suitcases......!

The waiting does have its benefits as our hotel is just around the corner from Naomi and Ian so we are able to see quite a lot of them, although we are trying very hard not to cramp their style! It is handy to have a readymade laundrette and a permanent parking permit for the car!

Stephen says he is on a very steep learning curve as he has never worked with coal before but so far he appears to be enjoying the new challenge. His office is just behind The Ritz and is only three stops on the underground from here - so very handy! I am enjoying the close proximity to Oxford Street which is only four stops and when necessary I can stop off and see Ian at work which is only two stops! The major dilemma now is where to live? It is unlikely that we will have to move to Australia at this time - but never say never!

So, there you have it; an update from the Lays. We will keep you informed, and maybe there will be some more tales to tell soon.

CAROL LAY

WANTED BY INTERPOL

Carol Lay

From:	Carol Lay
Sent:	17 August 2006 16:24
Subject:	Red Alert!

Hi Everybody

It is a long time since I last penned an email to you all, when you read the attached all will become clear! Whoever said life begins at 40 was clearly mistaken! At 50 it is time to "bring it all on"! - and what fun there is to be had!

We send you our best wishes, enjoy the summer and keep in touch

Love

Carol and (of course the 'editor-in-chief') Stephen

What ever happened to Australia? Red Alert!
Wednesday 16 August 2006

"Step this way, sir, I'm sure it's not serious......"
How wrong he was!

On Thursday, November 3rd 2005 Stephen and I flew from Moscow to New York to meet up with Tamsin, Naomi and Ian and to support Naomi in running the New York Marathon. We were very excited as we hadn't seen the children since early August. The flight had been uneventful and we were waiting our turn in the immigration queue, amused by the number of people being 'escorted' to a room behind the desks as their papers were not in order. Little did we expect that a few minutes later we would be in a far worse position!

The immigration control takes you through in your family group. My passport was duly stamped, fingerprint taken etc. and then Stephen's was put to one side. Next thing we knew we were being apologetically escorted to a waiting room. Apparently there were a few concerns regarding Stephen, the customs officer reassured us there was nothing to worry about.

What followed was a very frightening and uncomfortable couple of hours, it seemed much longer and now we realise it could have been so much worse. I was invited to stay with Stephen and as we watched all the eastern Europeans with inadequate or illegal papers and no English being merrily sent on their way we patiently sat there whilst whispered phone calls were made. At no time were we made aware of the problem other than Stephen was told there was a problem regarding unpaid taxes.

Eventually, they decided that due to time differences it was unlikely that the situation would be resolved before the next day and probably not until the beginning of the next week.

I was told to leave, Stephen was being detained.

I was escorted to collect the luggage and preparing to head for the hotel alone, armed with a long list of contact numbers and working out what to tell the children. Stephen was to remain in the holding room and would even be escorted to the toilet as and when necessary.

However, good sense finally resolved the situation and thankfully the USA officials announced "we do not have an extradition agreement with Georgia"! Stephen was free to leave the airport but was warned in no uncertain manner NOT to return in the future without obtaining a full visa.

We left as swiftly as possible and it was not really until we were in the taxi on the way to the hotel that the real enormity of the situation hit us and has since come back with a vengeance to haunt us and involves arrest warrants, Interpol etc.

And so a very complicated situation began to materialise, and it all began like this……

Once upon a time about eight years ago Stephen was Director of Finance and Operations of an Australian company with a gold mine in a faraway country called Georgia, the one that is part of the Former Soviet Union, not the one in the USA. And thereby hangs the tale!

Stephen is diligent, honest and hardworking and the Australian company he was working for were very lucky to have him! The team began to develop the gold project into the most successful foreign investment company in the country. They were producing good quantities of gold, improving the local economy and enriching the lives of the local community - in all an out and out success story.

In the immediate area of the mine the company was well respected as the only contributor to the local economy, and through creative thinking were able to contribute in other ways to the community. Stephen became prominent in the community and in Tbilisi. He met with President Shevardnadze on more than one occasion; was Chairman of a Division One Football Club, and was even known to drink a glass of cyanide solution (used in very low concentrations in the gold industry) to prove to the founder of the Green Party and Chairman of Parliament that it was harmless! (Georgian wine is far more dangerous!). We have even heard, recently, that he won "Best Foreign Businessman of the Year" in 2000, though he doubts the accuracy of this – he was certainly nominated.

However, nothing about working in the FSU is straightforward. Accepting and respecting that different countries and cultures have their own way of working is part of doing business in a foreign country, especially when you are the foreigner. Some things you can put up with or turn a blind eye to, and then there are other things which you just cannot and will not accept. Sometimes people become very greedy and as the breakaway FSU countries became more confident they also became more ruthless and less scrupulous. It is a fact that these countries conduct business dishonestly and corruptly as a way of life that is natural to them. Stephen is shrewd, and was aware of the ways the Georgians did business; and while he understood it was an inherent part of the way they did business, he was not prepared to succumb to underhand business practices, moreover, he was not prepared to risk either his own, nor the Australian company's, good and honest reputation. He was never, ever, corrupt, dishonest or committed anything illegal.

The Georgian authorities were extremely corrupt and a law unto themselves. They pride themselves on their independence. They are fighters, having warded off their near neighbours and being on the Silk Route they consider themselves to be on the trading crossroads. Whether this method of working is the result of all this, has been forced upon them because of the outfall of communism or is because they choose to live in this way is a question for greater philosophers and historians than me.

If asked, Stephen would unquestionably state that working for the Australian company in Georgia was, and to date remains, the highlight of his career. Sadly, it was to end in a very unfortunate manner.

I will reminisce a little! Stephen and I celebrated the Millennium in Tiblisi, Georgia. We flew in a couple of days before New Year and as we arrived at the airport, before we had even cleared immigration, visa control etc. etc. Stephen was apprehended by two large Georgians physically demanding money from him. By "physically" I mean exactly that, they restrained Stephen bending his arms behind his back whilst they made their demand and while I looked on. The Georgians are a race renowned for their warmth of welcome!! However, Stephen's own 'heavies' were soon on the scene and the situation was 'amicably' resolved and we were soon at our hotel where the following day we received two extremely expensive tickets to the Millennium celebrations from one of the men who had tried to extract money the previous evening!

I think this probably marked the beginning of the end.

As the mine became more successful, so the local Mafia wanted to increase their share of the success to the extent that they tried on more than one occasion to take over the operation and evict Stephen. They tried every trick they knew and despite Stephen's best effort to be one step ahead and out-think them - they continued to have the upper hand as they had the power to make, break and change the rules - at a whim!

Ultimately and despite his personal twenty four hour a day bodyguards, Stephen's life was under threat and he was pulled out of the country. A sad day for him, the Australian company and all the Georgians who had been employed in the project. The Georgians took management control and within a few months gold production had stopped.

And so you may be forgiven for thinking the story was at an end, an unfortunate end, but nevertheless an end. So did Stephen and I!

This brings us back to the beginning of November 2005 and Stephen's detention at JFK airport. It was difficult to obtain any clear reasons for the problem from the Immigration officials but Stephen managed a quick glance at the notes regarding the enquiries and saw the word "Interpol"! Naturally, following this debacle Stephen began to make some investigations of his own but despite some rummaging and question asking it was not until March this year that the proverbial really hit the fan.

You already know that in March Stephen accepted the post of CEO of the company with the Australian coal deposits. It was two days later that the severity of the situation then became apparent.

Stephen joined the new company on March 20th. Their only resource is in Australia which meant travelling there and a great deal of international travel. On March 22nd Stephen applied for his visa to Australia, and lo and behold there was a problem - not a small technical hitch but an extremely scary, career and potentially life changing crisis.

The reason Stephen had been detained in New York was because he had charges against him from his time in Georgia BUT that was not all, he had an Interpol Red Notice against his name putting him in the same category of WANTED as Al Qaeda and the Taliban! The Australian Immigration Authority said he was "a person of concern" and would not be allowed into their country until the Interpol notice was removed. This was despite numerous and lengthy testimonials and affidavits supporting Stephen - and the fact that while he was in Georgia he was doing business for an Australian company and had the support of the Australian Ambassador - they still preferred to believe an extremely corrupt country.

In his new position Stephen was put in an untenable position, he was at risk of arrest if he left the UK (even in the UK) and could not travel to Australia where the focus of business was. He had no choice, but to resign his post and is now 'retired' with me......

Since, with good legal support in Georgia and diplomatic help from the British Embassy in Tbilisi, Stephen has, we think, had the charges dropped, although we have still received no written evidence in support of this.

Three weeks ago we heard from the Australian Commission that the Red Notice has both been dropped and the diffusion notice issued to all countries. The Australian Immigration Department has informed Stephen that as he is no longer "a person of concern" they will issue him a visa. We are still awaiting its arrival!

So, the story has a happy ending and possibly a moral. Although Stephen is slightly bitter regarding his treatment by the Australian Authorities he has no regrets about his time in Georgia. Doing good business anywhere is difficult these days, to feel you have succeeded and carried out good business in a country where there is scant regard to honesty is certainly an achievement to be justly proud of despite the personal cost. But Stephen is alive, well, and has already received several job offers. We have no immediate plans to go to Australia in the near future and it is only because we have two very dear friends there, one of whom has been a real support to Stephen in this very difficult time that we may visit one day.

So, if you had been wondering why you had not received the next volume of "Journeys with My Husband" from Australia, you now know! You can also say you know somebody who was on a very much "WANTED" list. The book is in the offing so John Le Carre you have been warned - the truth is far more scary than fiction!

We have had an unsettling few months but are now looking forward to "chilling", I think they call it! Take care

Carol and Stephen

STOP PRESS:

On Thursday 17th August 2006 Stephen received a telephone call from the Australian High Commission to inform him that he had been granted permission to obtain a visa to visit Australia!

ABOUT THE AUTHOR

Carol Lay
1954 - 2017

Both Carol and Stephen Lay were brought up in Cornwall in South West England. They met at Helston School in 1970.

Carol graduated from a Teacher Training College in Hertfordshire and Stephen from the Camborne School of Mines in Cornwall.

They married in 1976. Three days later Carol started her first job as a special needs teacher. A year later Stephen graduated and started working in the local tin mines. They continued to live in West Cornwall.

Carol was committed to pushing the boundaries for her severely handicapped students, many achieving far more than could ever be imagined. The children, their parents and the teaching staff adored "mslay" with her boundless energy and keen sense of fun. In 1996 she won the South West England Teacher of the Year award in recognition of her work.

She gained a Master of Education degree and headship qualifications before retiring in 2005 to accompany Stephen, who since 1993 had been travelling extensively on various mining assignments.

Carol remained committed to helping young people, regardless of their ability, to achieve their potential and was trustee of several local charities and a committed Rotarian.

They have three children and five grandchildren.

Carol did not survive her battle against cancer. After a short and very dignified fight she died on 13th February 2017. She is lovingly remembered and very much missed.